F○CUS

Follow One Course Until Successful

TANIKA EVANS

F CUS

Follow One Course Until Successful

Copyright © 2022 by **Tanika Evans**

ISBN: 978-1-7372548-7-4

Daughter of the King Publishing

About the Author

Tanika Evans is a loving mom, and a wonderful and inspiring wife to Minister Brian Evans. The author has a BSc. in Business Communications & Management and is also a Certified & Accredited Life Coach, CEO & Founder of her Aesthetics & Beauty Business.

I'm very humorous, I am a hard worker, I am self-sufficient, I am a perfectionist, I am a fighter and I'm very determined.

I was born in Queens, New York in 1979 at LaGuardia Hospital to my devoted parents Linda and Tony. I was inspired to become an entrepreneur at a very young age, and that goal has been successfully accomplished since my early twenties.

I have two beautiful, amazing sons; my oldest is twenty three (23) years old and my youngest son is fifteen (15) years old. They both have two very different and witty personalities.

Being a leader by heart, it is my desire to embody that role in service to others and my community. It is my desire to help people achieve greatness by pursuing their dreams and to help them create a vision and ideas for their future.

I've conquered so much in my life; I've overcome being hurt, disappointed, let down and discouraged through a lot of pain. However despite all that I was challenged with,

I was able to graduate college and be an example for my children. I focused on myself, found my identity, created a path of consistency but most importantly surrendered my life to Christ.

It was through those hurdles that God's plan for my life began to unfold. God ordained the meeting of me and my husband. In God's timing he was sent into my life so that we could build a beautiful life together.

"As for me and my house, we will serve the Lord."

God is the reason why I succeeded; He is the reason I was able to push forward. Throughout each and every hurdle, throughout all the hurt and pain, my relationships with my children's fathers, and my enemies who were trying to pull me down, God lifted me up and gave me the strength to keep moving forward.

It was very difficult, but I'm ambitious and I chose to stay the course.

One of the hardest things in life is to not know who you really are. But it gets easier when you can identify your true identity. That's the hardest thing in life to overcome.

I don't regret any of it; there is "pain in purpose." Some things in life have to happen for us to become who God created us to be. It was all apart of God's plan for my life.

I will never stop moving. I will never give up because I know that God will always be there to back me up.

Ultimately, I've always been able to make a comeback, reinvent myself and stay relevant.

"I believe that progress is not for the faint of heart."

Introduction

I wrote this book because I believe God has a purpose and plan for every life, and while we pursue it, we're going to go through things along the way. Many times I cried out to God asking Him why I was going through a situation and wondered if He could get me out of it. I didn't realize then that what I was going through was part of His plan. He ordained it to happen.

The process of seeking God's face and walking by faith and not by sight has to be a desire deep within an individual.

God wants you to open your eyes, and see that He will unapologetically remove you from your comfort zone. He does this to take you to a new level that you are not ready for, so that you would understand that He is God.

We should never idolize man more than we idolize God. We are all His children. He loves us. He loves the good and the bad. But we are going to go through unpredictable storms. Speaking as a woman of faith, the weapons may form, but they will not prosper against those who believe.

Sometimes the things we manifest are things we create on our own, and do not always appear because of someone else. I want this book to bring out the lion in you; the you that God created you to be. One who can cast out fear, rebuke the devil and realize your dreams and goals. If I can do it, so can you.

Essentially, nothing improves until we improve. Therefore we have to want to change ourselves before we can see a solution. I had to finally take a long look in the mirror at myself and say:

"Whatever it is I want, wants me."

"Whatever it is you want, wants you."

I'm sure there are a lot of people who can relate to me when it comes to fulfilling a dream or an idea in their lives. Sometimes we let the connection with our consciousness shut down and allow the negative things we think about to reflect on the outside. That is a pure negative vibe and negative energy. When we have a dream or an idea that we wish to bring to life, why shut it down over and over again? Because we believe we can't make it happen. God placed that dream in our hearts. He placed the desire for that dream in our minds for a reason.

I've personally heard that negative voice tearing my dreams and visions down for years, saying to me "You're going to fail if you do that. Don't even think about it. It's not going to happen; continue doing what you've been doing."

Nothing in my life is ever going to function properly unless I have a renewed mind-set.

I believe in healing, but broken focus never succeeds. That is very important to know and to understand. People are going to continue to deny who you are. They will deny your greatness, but the negative people are not attached to your destiny.

When I first became an entrepreneur in my twenties (20's), I was honestly living and learning a lot about myself; I made some mistakes, but I also discovered that I had a talent and a gift. Therefore I worked toward developing my craft.

There were certainly times when that voice in my mind tried to shatter my confidence, when I allowed it.

That's the voice we normally hear in the morning, throughout our day and evening that makes us feel like we didn't accomplish everything that we needed to. When that negative voice turns on in your mind, immediately turn that negative thought into a positive thought. Say to yourself:

"I'm not doing this to myself today."

"Today is going to be a positive and productive day. Every day is a new day to be a better day."

So to you my dear readers, if that is you, I'm here to tell you, those thoughts and voices in your mind are absolutely not of God. It is a lie from the pit of hell. The enemy wants you to fear, stress and worry about everything; the devil is a liar.

"If God is for you who can be against you?" Romans 8:31.

Imagine purchasing your first home, your dream car or that business that you always wanted to start…

Or even something that you saved up for that you bought all on your own…

How would you use the keys from your past to open new doors in your future?

"Old Keys Don't Unlock New Doors."

Table of Contents

CHAPTER 1

Foundation of Family

The eye cannot say to the hand, "I don't need you!" And the head cannot say to the feet, "I don't need you!" 1 Corinthians 12:21

God created a man and a woman in His perfect image. He created the female to be perfect for the male, and He created the male to be perfect for the female. In today's society both men and women always seem to expect each other to do everything in the same way; to behave in the same way, to think in the same way, and to react in the same way. Why is that? In reality people honestly don't understand and appreciate their God-given differences. And that is what eventually creates conflict. God has given specific strengths to the female that the male cannot possess and vice versa. Until both the man and the woman can recognize the creativity God has placed within each of them, they will continue to be weak in certain areas because they were purposely designed to supply what the other lacks. The woman and the man have two very different strengths and neither will ever be able to function properly without the other.

When we understand and value each other's purpose, we can appreciate a rewarding relationship, and two people can blend their unique designs in a beautiful way for God's glory.

I was born a Virgo on September 10, 1979 at LaGuardia Hospital in Queens NY. I was born during the most beautiful era - the late 70s into the 80s. It was an innocent era where disco reigned supreme, and everyone was wearing afros, crazy haircuts to look hip, and hairstyles for women that made them very classy. Many of the 70s fashion trends have earned permanent positions in today's fashion. Women like Farrah Fawcett, Diana Ross, Pam Grier, Cleopatra Jones and Diahann Carroll had a relaxed elegance about themselves in the 70s.

I was born during the time when people actually listened to cassettes on the go and eight tracks in the 80s. I never really knew what eight tracks were actually for, but there was something about being able to flip over a cassette to the other side in your radio, or hold an album cover in your hand while walking down the street, that made music feel more special and personal in the 80s. People relied on good music in my era growing up. The 80s was the era of bright, bold and big. Both men and women were compelled by the beauty industry. Fitness, nutrition and the natural physique of a woman in the 80s encouraged athletically toned bodies, bodysuits and tracksuit bottoms. Some of the most beautiful women in the 80s were Brooke Shields, Sade, Madonna and Lisa Bonet.

As a child I grew up singing and dancing to artist like Whitney Houston. She was one of my favourite singers as a young girl, and my soul adapted to her music from a very young age. It always made me happy and put me to sleep. I love to dance as well, and my mom would always tell stories as I got older about how I loved music as well as eating. When I was a baby my family had a nickname for me; they called me chubby because I loved food, and I still do to this day. It makes sense seeing how I love singing in my car, I love singing in the shower, and I especially love singing praise and worship music in my home and at church. Music gives me peace. This is who I am; it's a part of my personality. It actually runs in my family because my grandfather loves to sing in church, my mom loves singing and dancing and so do my two sons.

My oldest loves singing and playing music just like me. I remember vividly one hot sunny day I was very young. I was riding in the car with my parents and godparents. I had to be about maybe three or four years old. I was sitting in the backseat of the car in my car seat and we were on our way to the beach while a song played on the radio by Tina Marie called Square biz. My mom turned around and looked at me and smiled. I was in my seat with my kitty beach glasses on, singing my little heart out with my eyes closed and bopping my head to the beat. Everyone just turned around and looked at me. They started laughing because they thought it was so adorable.

Having a childhood to remember is a beautiful thing. I remember my brother and I growing up being only four years apart. We spent a significant amount of time together getting on each other's nerves. Being the oldest, I loved to play mommy. Sometimes I would dress him and brush his hair. He hated to get his hair brushed. I remember some of our favourite shows were Mr. Rogers. We used to watch The Cosby Show, Annie, Soul Train, and one of my brothers favourites- ThunderCats. He would literally sit and watch that cartoon after school every day. It got to the point where I would then sit and watch it with him, and it became one of our favourite cartoons to watch together. I remember my mom getting him the little figurines from the cartoon, and we wrestled. I got my first cabbage patch on Christmas one year. It was the little things like that made us kids very happy.

Kids today would actually laugh at how video games were played back in the day. We had to pay a quarter every time we played each game. It made the experience way more fun, personal and it wasn't a competitive thing. We didn't just sit in our homes and flip the consul endlessly; we had to eventually save up money to walk to the store or play the video games at the arcade. I have a lot of cool memories growing up as a kid. Being the first born child amongst my two siblings for the first four years of my life was memorable. I remember being spoiled as the firstborn grandchild by my grandmother and my aunts. I kind of just got passed around to everyone individually, to love on me in their own way and I became very attached to them. I really didn't go to a lot of people when I was little, but when I saw the relevant people I knew well, my face always lit up.

After my siblings were born years later, the party was over. I was no longer the center of attention who got everything she wanted all the time. My mother had my brother and my little sister, and my aunts eventually had children as well. So I wound up being almost 10 years older than my cousins. In the same way that me and my youngest aunt are 10 years apart today. When I was born, my youngest aunt was about nine or 10 years old. I remember my mom telling me stories about how excited her younger sisters were the day that she went into labour because they knew they were getting the day off from school. As I got older my aunts became more like my sisters, especially the youngest one. I think that's why at times we didn't get along. My mom literally gave me her name but just added the letter k to it. We were blessed as a family to always be so close, and to kind of grow up in the same house together. Even if we were not living together, we weren't too far away from each other.

My mom walked the streets as a beautiful woman. When she was younger she was short about 5 5". She had good textured hair, light skin, beautiful lips and features with a curvy petite physique. She loved wearing jeans, a white tee and sneakers. Everyone used to tell her she looked like Sade, who was known in the 80s as one of the most beautiful women in the music industry. I remember my mom having a sense of humour when I was a kid. I grew up around some of her closest friends, one of which is my godmother today.

Years later after my parents separated, and my mom had my siblings with their dad, she eventually became a single mom to the three of us. As a child I remember watching my mom do her hair, cook dinner, clean the house and help us with homework- but most importantly I remember always being very passionate about creating a life and a path for myself which I do remember was hard for her at times. It seemed as though she struggled with understanding the principle behind her purpose, and she struggled to add value to her life no matter what came her way. That mindset, of course, was passed down to my siblings and I until we became adults. At some point we realized that everyone has a formula for their lives which they typically allow to work for them. But the question that we began to ask ourselves was: what was her actual formula? My mom is actually an amazing woman. She's funny, she has a great heart and she loves people with all that she has. She raised my siblings and I and did the absolute best she could our whole life.

Growing up as a child, I found that my mom was very similar to me. She was a very humble child. She never asked for much, or expected my grandparents to give her expensive things as a teen. She was happy with what they bought her. However growing up around my grandmother and my aunts, I realized that there was favouritism in my family with my mother's sisters. When this is something that a child sees, feels, hears and knows, it causes anger and behavioural problems- increased levels of depression, a lack of confidence in themselves and a refusal to interact well with others. Children eventually become a part of their . These issues appear in children who are favoured by a parent as well as those who are not. Love and attention are the most important things a child needs from both of their parents.

For those of you who are parents reading this book, I'm sure you have that one child who you feel is the golden child, but the other children should not be aware of it. They should feel equally loved. And I had to learn this very important principle when I became a mom myself. My children are eight years apart, so the love, affection and attention I gave them individually was at two very different levels of my life because of the age gap between the two of them. Being a mom at two completely different times while discovering my own identity was challenging for me.

As a young girl, I noticed my aunts dealing with favouritism. My grandmother had four daughters and they all love her very much. Sometimes being a parent can be difficult. I don't think any parents who bring children into the world want their kids to feel neglected or unloved. Sometimes it could be easier to parent one child than the other, or perhaps one child may be easier to be around than the other. Or another child may not have the same needs and struggles as the other. Maybe one child is really good at being a peacemaker, and the other is loud and obnoxious. There are many reasons why a parent or parents may show favouritism towards one child over the others, but it is the parents responsibility for the children to have an individual bond with them in some way no matter what. By the grace of God, we were always able to live in middle class neighbourhoods with decent schools, and safe environments for the most part of my life.

I remember being in kindergarten and having a good relationship with my teachers. I was always a very good girl in school. Like my mom, I never gave my teachers any problems. I remember abiding by the rules in class, and I just wasn't a complicated kid. I was a very good listener in school. My teachers would put all the children in groups, and when it was time to do a project, they would always pair me with other kids to bring out the personalities of my classmates. I remember being the person that would possibly be the one to raise my hand for us, or to speak first if I had something to say.

I have always been very outspoken. I was not shy in elementary school. I kind of just had the kind of personality that stood out. I was always very quiet until somebody asked me a question, or wanted to share their snack with me, and at that moment I felt it was my opportunity to bring out the best in others as a leader. I love to help people; I always kind of did my own thing as a leader and not a follower. I loved and enjoyed arts and crafts when I was younger. Today that is my sister's gift. She is an amazing artist and has the kind of talent that could be recognized nationally. That girl can draw. She is very gifted. I truly believe that you can do whatever you put your mind to. We all have the ability and the power to manifest whatever it is that you want in your life.

My childhood years throughout elementary and middle school consisted of my siblings and I growing up in Suffolk County, Brentwood NY. We played outside as kids until the street lights came on, we enjoyed riding bikes with our friends, playing hide and seek and double dutch. My brother loves basketball, and we would even play baseball outside in the front yard with our friends from across the street. We always- made up our own games outside. we played hopscotch in the street with chalk and we would use rocks to play hopscotch. We enjoyed our childhood, and then Nintendo came out and it was over.

Elementary school was when I really started to acknowledge some of my talents. Gymnastics was really amazing for me because I was very athletic, and in sixth grade I won a trophy. I was the happiest little girl. I remember my mom and dad came to my first gymnastic show, and my dad bought me some flowers and we all went out to eat together at Sizzler afterwards. I was so excited that he came to my gymnastic show. I didn't think my dad was going to come, but my mom surprised me as she called him and they both showed up together. It turned out to be one of the most amazing days for me as a young girl. We took pictures with my teacher and my friends, and it was a memorable moment.

My gymnastic teacher loved me; she used to tell me I was very flexible in stretching. I was great on the balance beam doing backhand springs, and it taught me how to focus and how to test my faith. That was a very important time in my life because I had to challenge myself after school every day. To excel to the next level it takes a lot of discipline. I always had a sense of fear in me somehow, and I never knew where that really came from. I was always very afraid of dogs growing up, and because of that fear, eventually as an adult I got bit by a pitbull. There was a very good part of me that had a lot of faith in myself, and I had this lion personality that made me feel like a leader, but then there was another side of me that always demonstrated a lot of fear. It took me a long time to discover where that came from.

I was always afraid of dogs growing up as a child and it made me not like dogs. The sight of a dog coming up to me while I was walking on the street, or if I saw a dog anywhere near my existence made my heart race and it put a sense of fear in me. Maybe it could've been because my mother never had animals in the house when we were growing up. I was never around dogs, and so I never knew how to allow a dog to sense who I am to build a rapport and a loving relationship with me. I had experienced that in the world on my own and it was a very scary feeling. I think my mom may have unknowingly passed that down to me, but as I got older I overcame it. I realized that if I could do something, it made me want to do better. It made me want to do more in life.

Not only was I in gymnastics but I ran track in high school and I was in competitions. My coach put me as a top runner on the track and field team, and I did it to challenge myself. It was different from a competing perspective in middle school with gymnastics. My coach thought I was amazing; the perfect person to run on the track. I won ribbons and medals for racing with my team. I was hard-working from a very young age, and being put in those positions made me who I am today. It fit my personality as well as my characteristics.

Swimming was also another thing that I was afraid of until I overcame that fear by teaching myself how to swim. I spent a lot of time with my cousins growing up in Long Island, and there was a pool in the backyard of my grandmothers twin sisters house. All of those hot summer days that we spent in the pool until our feet and hands turn wrinkly. It turned me into an excellent swimmer. I learned how to float, kick my feet, hold my breath under the water and eventually jump off the diving board into a 10 feet deep pool. That was an awesome day.

By the way my mom almost had a heart attack. She had no clue that I knew how to swim. When she saw me up on the diving board as she was laughing and talking with the family, all I heard was her screaming saying, "No get down from there right now!" Everyone was looking, so I just jumped off the diving board into the pool and surfaced right back up from under the water. I started to swim to the other side of the pool into 5 feet and she was amazed. Her jaw hit the floor, and she ran over to me with a towel and said, "Oh my God you almost gave me a heart attack." "Great job I had no idea you learned how to swim." What my mom didn't know was, even though she always told me to stay in the shallow end of the pool where I could stand up and not drown, there were ropes in the water that separated the deep end from the 5ft shallow end. She never really worried about me playing in the pool because the shallow end had less water. Thankfully my cousins taught me how to swim when she thought we were just playing. So it was great. I can get in water no matter how deep it is and survive.

Being the oldest child made me very overprotective towards my siblings- especially my brother because we were only a few years apart and I've always played the big sister role with him. I was like a little mommy towards them. I remember my sister being in the house most of the time with my mom because she was a baby. My mother's sisters eventually had children around the same time my sister was born, so my sister had my cousins to be around and to play with. My brother and I were just so much older than her. I had cousins on my dad's side as well, but I really wasn't that close to my dad's family because of the separation with my parents and how far apart we all lived.

I do remember there was a time when my mom let me go down south with my paternal grandmother during the summer, and that was really the only interaction I've ever had with my father's mother. She loved me very much. She cherished the time that my mother allowed her to spend with me during that summer vacation. I enjoyed myself with her. I met another little girl around my age while I was visiting and we became friends over the summer. It's very hot down south, and back in those days people lived in trailers that looked like houses.

My grandmother had a very nice trailer that looked exactly like a house that she lived in. I was shocked because I had never saw a trailer until I went to spend the summer with her. It had everything: a kitchen a living room, bathrooms, bedrooms and a dining room. It was like being in a house but instead I spent the summer in a trailer. I thought that was very cool. My paternal grandmother who is in her 80s, is now in a nursing home due to an accident she had which led to a stroke. She needed to be cared for. I haven't seen her since I was a little girl, but I have spoken to her over the phone and she knows I love her. I really didn't get a chance to spend any more time with her after that summer vacation.

I grew up being close to my maternal grandmother whom I was very attached to growing up. My maternal grandmother has a twin sister, a younger sister and a brother. They all have children. My mom is very close to her cousins, so my family is very big. I have first, second and third generations of cousins, and we all love each other very much. My maternal grandmother spent a lot of time with her twin sister as I was growing up in Long Island, so there were many gatherings with us as a large family together. We were tight knit. My dad himself was in my life but in and out of the picture a lot. As I got older and became a woman, he became very attached and overprotective. He watched everyone that I was in a relationship with very carefully for my protection. I'm his only daughter and baby girl, and I know I can count on him. All it takes is a phone call. We're very close today.

When my parents separated my dad still had a lot of love for my mother. She was his first love and they were from Queens. Everyone knew not to mess with my mom or anyone in my family. My dad was very well known in his neighbourhood. He remained very close with my mom and her sisters after they separated, and we became a blended family during holidays and special occasions. There was never any hesitation to invite my dad to a function.

First Church Of God In Christ is my grandfather's church. He is a superintendent for his district in Glen Cove New York. My grandfather has been a Pastor for over 40 years. He is committed, dedicated and loyal to his church, his members and his community. My mother grew up going to church on weekends with my grandfather. He would put pretty dresses on her, put bows in her hair and cute little patent leather shoes. She would sit in church, clap her hands and dangle her feet for hours until she fell asleep.

My grandfather was a great father to his children, but he and my grandmother did not get along. After they divorced, he eventually remarried a Christian woman of faith, and his wife became very close with my mom, her sisters, and all of his grandchildren for over 40 years. She unfortunately passed a few years ago and it was a tremendous loss for our family. She was truly a woman of God who covered each and every one of my family members in prayer her entire life.

She covered us in prayer when we were sleeping, throughout our marriages, throughout our children being born and throughout all of the trials and tribulations that families go through. She was a praying woman. I never heard her curse in my entire life. She was not a worldly woman, but a true first lady who represented my grandfather with grace, dignity and respect. As a wonderful Pastor at First Church of God in Christ, my grandfather spent all of his life seeking God. He focused on being a great leader and participating with his support in the district of Glen Cove.

I attended church as a child but it wasn't consistent. My mom would take us to church as children on a Sunday if she needed to be lifted, or if she wanted to be filled with the spirit or God's love. We attended church when invited by my grandfather to his church for birthday celebrations, church anniversaries and holidays, but I don't remember us being members. My mom had her struggles throughout life like any other single mom, and at one point she did give her life to Christ. She got baptized, filled with the Holy Spirit with the initial evidence of speaking in tongues.

It was great seeing a change in her and the consistency with discovering her true identity, but somehow the enemy knew how to attack the mind of my family bloodline so it was not a consistent Christian lifestyle. Although her father is a Pastor, he lived a very private lifestyle and was extremely focused on himself and his church reputation after he separated from my grandmother. Growing up, I remember my mom and my aunt calling him when I was a child for help with various things going on in their lives, and he would always end the conversation telling them "I will pray for you have a nice day."

The women in my family always had a survival mindset with very tough skin, but they lacked inner balance within themselves and outer boundaries. Looking back, growing up in my house no one ever really told me the importance of God's love as a child. I knew of God because of the conversations and the things that I've heard in my family, and in church growing up but we never lived that life. I discovered all of this on my own.

CHAPTER 2

Becoming Me

And if my people who are called by my name will humble themselves and pray and seek my face and turn from their wicked ways then I will hear from heaven and will forgive their sin and will heal their land (2 Chronicles 7:14

Between middle school and high school I got acquainted with my identity a little bit more. I noticed that I really didn't want to be like my friends. I wasn't into wearing makeup and boys so much like they were, but of course I did look here and there at certain boys. I really didn't get into liking boys until eighth or ninth grade, and even then I would just talk to them, but they were really annoying and weird to me.

Throughout high school I was into sports and track. I really did well in high school. I was a good student and I got good grades. I always tried to focus on making my mom proud of me and my report card. That was very important to me because she was a single mom and she took good care of us. Failing in school was the last thing I wanted her to have to worry about, so doing well and making her happy was a priority to me.

My childhood taught me a lot about who I was, and how I achieved things without even really realizing it . When I got to 10th grade, I started being a little bit more rebellious, wanting to be the opposite of how I used to be in middle school. As you get older you start to develop your own opinions of the world. Although I started to hang out a little bit more with my peers, I never did any of the extreme things or picked up the habit of smoking cigarettes or smoking marijuana or anything like that. I hated the smell of cigarettes growing up, and so did the circle of girls I graduated high school with.

We were all pretty decent well behaved girls and we're still best friends to this day. We all worked at McDonald's. That was my first job at 16 which was great, but I realized as I was working there it wasn't enough money. I just wasn't happy with the amount of money I was making per hour deep down inside, so I wanted to go and get another job a year later working at Checkers.

I had enough money as a teenager to do what teenagers do; hang out at the mall, get my hair and nails done and hang out with my friends. My mom started to realize that I was working more than I was home, and she asked me where I was getting all this money from. I told her that I had another job. I always had a mentality to want more for myself, but of course as a mom, my mother wanted me to focus on school and not work so hard for money. She knew I was very responsible, so she kept an eye out on my grades and allowed me to continue working my senior year.

I graduated high school in 1997 with pretty decent grades. I did well enough to apply for college and that is exactly what I intended to do. During my senior year I had a boyfriend. He was already in college while I was a senior in high school. We hung out a lot. He played football in his senior year so we had a lot in common. We both lived in Long Island NY. He was an only child and lived in the same home with his parents from a very young age.

Our relationship grew stronger the more we hung out. He taught me how to drive and he was my date for my senior prom. His parents bought him a brand new car when he graduated high school, so he was very well-known in our neighbourhood. Driving a red Honda Civic with rims on it, he got a lot of attention from girls back then. We shared a certain kind of first love that I never experienced before. I guess the kind of love he had for me was the kind of love my father gave me as well, so that meant a lot to me.

I really didn't understand what love was and we were very young. He took me to Six Flags Great Adventure for the weekend after my prom, and I began preparing myself for college. As I started filling out all of my paperwork for school and getting my schedule ready for classes, I discovered I was pregnant at 18. I had my son when I was 19, so I had to put my dreams on hold to have him. Whether I was ready or not, it was time for me to grow up, and at that point the grand time of my life began.

I wanted to start out with business in college. Initially when I went to register for school I really didn't know what I wanted to do, so I just decided to start out with liberal arts. But that never happened. I was becoming a mom.

SIN: To all of my teenage readers, if you are a teenage mom like I was, I want to take a moment to speak about having a child out of wedlock. Many of you don't have someone you can confide in who can give you the knowledge you need to become the best version of yourself.   Sin is a very serious thing, and we first must acknowledge the impact of sin in our lives. As the Bible says, " it is so prevalent", and our fallen nature causes many problems and misunderstandings in regard to our faith, obedience and prayers later in life. JAMES 1:21

So here I am continuing to persevere. I decided to put everything on a hold, and I was never able to start my first class of college. Being pregnant became my priority. I was disappointed in myself and I went into a state of depression.   In reality getting pregnant is supposed to be the most precious time of your life. My body changed and of course my relationship started to decline after a while, and that was a major change in my life. Of course I had the support of my parents, my grandparents and my family, but I was very disappointed in myself. The drive in me, the fight in me, the leader in me, the ambitious person in me had gotten lost for some reason.

I started to think to myself, "Oh my God! I'm gonna be a mom." I know nothing about being a mom and I went into a state of shock. I was always the quiet one in my family. I was a good girl so this was something that my family didn't expect to happen to me. I was around the same age that my mother gave birth to me, so history was definitely repeating itself. After discussing it with my family and praying, it was something that we all chose to commemorate and celebrate more than anything. Life is a blessing from God, and being a mom is something that is significant and very important to a woman, so I proceeded with my pregnancy.

I went to all of my doctor's appointments with my son's father. Of course towards the end, he was a 20 year old young guy and we had our differences, but at the same time, I realized it was time for us to put our priorities in order sooner rather than later to feed our son. So we had no choice but to grow up really fast. I had to get out there and get a job. I had to put my dreams on hold and I had to put my big girl panties on to provide and be a mom who could take care of her responsibilities- and that's exactly what I did.

I started out working. I got a customer service job at a Call Center and I did that for a little while, but soon I became unhappy with the money I was making there. So I decided to look in the newspaper and get into sales. I wanted to make good money, not just enough money. I found a sales job working with a publishing company.

I went for the interview that day and it was the best day of my life. I remember the day like it was yesterday. I was so nervous. The fear that morning drove me crazy and I didn't know why? I had that side to me that would allow negative thoughts to discourage me in a way that caused doubt at times. I think we have all experienced that in life. We're human. You just never know what kind of day we're going to have when we wake up in the morning, and what side of our brain you're going to be operating when you wake up. Whether it's in the positive or negative, in all reality, you have complete control over the way you think. I just didn't know that back then.

I've always had the mentality to do anything that I set my mind to do, but there was that side where I felt like I was cursed. There was a sense of doubt in my mind that morning saying to me, "I hope this works out today." Nevertheless it turned out wonderful. I went for the interview that day and I met with the owner of the company. He said, "You speak with such clarity in your voice, you have great communication skills and you read the script very well." You're gonna be great at this job. Congratulations you're hired! You start Monday."

From that day forward my life changed. I went from making $110 at McDonald's to making $600 a week, and I was only 20 years old. I was excited about all the things I could do for my son with this money. From that point on, I realized I wanted to stay in sales and be an entrepreneur, working on commission with no cap on my pay. As the years went on, I became very good at what I do. I landed top sale roles, setting huge examples for other employees and becoming a massive closer and trainer in the company. Of course I started to make way more money than I started off with, and I was able to negotiate with my bosses after being recruited to other companies doing the same thing. This led to more of a leadership role, and I began to develop an impeccable background and a fantastic reputation in sales.

Walking into the unknown of being a mom for the first time, and feeling somewhat outnumbered, I doubled a personality that elevated me. At one point even though I wasn't consistent and going to church, I did believe in God and having my son was the greatest gift God has ever given to me. My son was a beautiful child when he was born. I had a natural pregnancy with no medication. I was young so the labour pains were excruciating, but that was the most difficult part of my delivery.

My son was a little stubborn. He didn't want to come out when I was in labour, so it lasted for almost 16 hours. When it was time to push, I pushed him out and he just popped out like jelly. He was a beautiful baby. After my son was born into the world healthy, with 10 fingers and 10 toes, I observed him and was so proud of myself. He was beautiful- fair skin complexion similar to my mom, beautiful hair, dark brown eyes and the most beautiful lips

I've ever seen. It wasn't until about two weeks later that I discovered he had a birthmark on his forehead which didn't fully appear until after his complexion set in. Because he was very light when he was born, his birthmark was a little darker than his complexion. From that day on I knew my son was born to be a superstar.

I wanted to take full responsibility as a mom, and I honestly felt that I could never stop moving in the direction towards success with his life in my hands. I didn't want to give up all of my dreams, goals or visions that God placed in my heart. I knew I had to make motherhood my priority, so with that, I had to plan and strategize for our future.

Every decision I made from that point on was for his benefit. I had to really figure out how to reinvent myself every time someone tried to pull me down and stay relevant no matter what- and that's what I did. I never really cared about other people's opinion of me. I always took very good care of my son. I stayed to myself a lot and I kept him very clean, at all times. Anyone who ever ran into me in my neighbourhood and saw my son, always told me how groomed I always kept him and that he always smelled so good. I made sure he had everything he needed and put him before myself.

At this point I was making very good money and I was able to get my own apartment, so I no longer was living with my mother. Intelligence for me was based on perspective, and I had a lot of different opinions from many people in my life at such a young age. I realized that you can't trust someone with conflicting information, so I always reflected back to God. For some reason He was the only one who could give me peace. I kind of use that as my cloak of security, because I knew that God could give me strength to move forward more than anyone else.

I had a saying that I used to tell myself a lot. I would say, "Lord give me the strength to get through today." I had a hard time trusting others throughout my life. The only person I can rely on is myself, and if I was willing to be different, if I could see what others couldn't see, then I could do what others couldn't do. The most challenging thing for me was not being married, having a child out of wedlock, and not consulting any of that with God before it happened. I never consulted him before I made choices.

Most of my life was just me browsing through, without a care in the world, guiding myself through my own flesh. Now as a mother to two children I realize God knew all of this was going to happen in my life before I was even born. He knew all of my failures and all of my mistakes that I was going to make. He knew it all when I was in my mom's womb. None of it was a surprise to Him.

My two boys are eight years apart. I had my older son and then I didn't have my second son until eight years later. I was 26 years old when my second son was born. It still hindered me from doing what I dreamed and what I envisioned for myself without children, but I had to put them first. I had to think outside of the box. I didn't want to rely on anyone for anything. I guess you can say I was kind of stubborn, but I knew I couldn't get time back. We can't take back yesterday for today, so I focused on investing my time on a daily basis to work on making myself better and who I was created to be.

My primary concern was doing what I had to do as a mom, so when my older son was born, I breast-fed him for the first three years of his life. It required me to really want to know a lot about being a mom. I had no idea what being a mom consisted of but I wanted to do what was best for him. Breast milk contain antibodies that help your baby fight off viruses and bacteria. It also prevents your baby from having asthma and allergies, so this became a lifestyle for the first few years of his life. For all of you mom's reading my book, I'm sure you know the longer you breast-feed your child, the longer your milk produces in your breast. I had to wean him off slowly but surely at the age of four years old, so that the milk would stop producing in my breast. He was very attached to me and I had to work.

Parenting is a huge responsibility. If you don't know who you are, you can go down the wrong path and you can be influenced by other people who don't have the same mindset as you. I had to take a really long look at myself in the mirror to understand that I have a sense of self-control, confidence and my own identity. I thank God for my mother because if it wasn't for her giving me that sense of sanity, and taking my son off my hands on the weekends, I wouldn't have free time to myself to just be a normal 20 year old girl. Because of her, I did not have to worry about feedings, pampers, napping and paying bills. It was a relief to get a break and to just be a 20 year old sometimes on the weekend.

When you become a mother you come second to your child. You're not the priority anymore, and that was something that I understood very well. Some of you may be teen moms and you don't know how to do that so you become very depressed. If you become a single mom, it can take a toll on you. I actually know of a girl that killed both of her kids. She gave herself two choices after suffering from severe depression: either they lived or she would. She killed her twin babies and ruined her entire life, because she suffered from postpartum depression.

Being a mother requires patience, mental stability, love and nurturing for your child. When you work and you're a mom at the same time, it's a lot. When you're young and in a relationship, and your partner wants attention as well, it's crucial to build each other up. I thank God for my friends who supported me when I got pregnant. It felt good to have friends who were there for me when both my children were born. I had the most amazing baby shower for my firstborn son. My mom and my son's father's family gave me the most beautiful baby shower. My son did not need anything until he was about three years old. He didn't want or need anything.

Being an entrepreneur required me to have a lot of confidence. I worked very closely with top producers in my industry which enhanced my skills throughout the years as a Senior Editor. I was selling top memberships to professionals and executives all over the world. They were from various industries and occupations, and I've done this in a very prestigious magazine for exposure and recognition. I've seen a lot of people come and go in the sales industry, but maintaining your credibility as a top producer can be a very challenging position.

Just like anything else in sales, the game changes every day. You have to be creative, you have to be confident and you have to have your own enthusiasm and motivation on a daily basis. My sales career gave me an explosive entrepreneurial mindset which later motivated me to have multiple streams of income. I started to develop a natural instinct for flipping my own money into other projects. I didn't realize it then, but I do know the rules to my success were: don't stop, own your dreams and love what you do. I had to become my best self by using my own uniqueness. I didn't despise or regret any of my small beginnings because it made me who I am today. When you're in alignment with your will it's ok to take things step-by-step.

And it's ok to be hidden, because when God is ready to reveal you on the scene you won't be like everybody else. You will be you. People will appreciate you for your uniqueness and who you are. I started to have fun in the process of finding myself and enjoying every experience on the ride. Be a student of life. Find a reason every day to write down what you can improve on from the day before. Have faith, because everything in life that you go through can work out for your good, if you let it be of light to help someone else.

CHAPTER 3

Life is Ordained by God

If any of you lacks wisdom he should ask God who gives generously to all without finding fault and it will be given to him, but when he asks he must believe and not doubt, because he who doubts is like a wave of the sea blown and tossed by the wind, that man should not think he will receive anything from the Lord; he is a double minded man unstable and all he does. James 1:5-8

I want my readers to know that discovering your identity and knowing your purpose is extremely important. We can only go so far as humans in life on our own without having some form of connectedness or alignment with God. We were created by Him, so there's nothing that we should want to do in this life without Him.

Life is a gift, and it offers us the privilege, opportunity and responsibility to give something back by becoming more than what we think we are. In order for that to happen, we have to somewhat identify who we are at some point and everybody's journey is going to be different. I am someone who went through a lot of devastating challenges in my life, but as a fighter I was determined to never give up. Why? Because I'm not clothes, I don't fold. I always pushed myself to continue moving forward. When you give up, the enemy wins. You have to embrace who you are becoming, and know that the challenges you're going through are just a test. You're actually just passing through a difficult moment of life. You have to understand that you have to embrace it during the process, even when you don't know what the outcome is going to be.

Both of my children's fathers helped me identify who I really was, because I was experiencing these uncomfortable stages at two separate ages of my life years apart. My experience with each of them was very similar, but different in a variety of ways. There was a lot of love there, but when you're young and you're in a relationship with the wrong people, you're not mature enough to acknowledge it's time to let it go. Their ups and downs become your ups and downs. Neither one of them were assigned to my life for God's purpose, so it didn't last the way I wanted it to. It was a chapter in a season that I experienced, and it was a wonderful experience because I matured and realized those chapters were over.

If someone wants to walk out of your life, let them go. You will always be who God says you are, not man. The reason I couldn't let go of my relationship when it was very clear we were not supposed to be together, was because of the image of us I planted in my mind of having a family. I put more value into those relationships than I did in God. I made them more of a priority than I did God. Once your mindset changes, everything else in your life will change right along with it.

My first relationship was right out of high school. My experience was wonderful in the beginning. It was young love, but as you grow, especially with a child involved in the situation, people change and the situation changes. We didn't understand the requirements of adulthood and being a parent at the same time. I tried my very best to make it work in both my relationships, but I definitely lost myself in the process and I stayed longer than I should have. My destiny was not attached to their souls.

I had my second son with his father at the age of 26. There were very high expectations in my second relationship. I was already on my own. I had my own apartment, a good job and reliable transportation for me and my son. He had a very good job as well working for the Department of Sanitation, but was living at home with his mother in Queens. Financially we were able to take care of our son. Although that relationship did not work out after a few years, we both moved on to work on ourselves. I had requirements and expectations from him, but sometimes people will disappoint you and you have to accept the fact that someone else's plans to prosper may not include you. Over a long period of time, people change and the reason I finally left my ex was because we were very toxic, and someone was going to end up dead if we continued to stay together.

Once I know somebody doesn't want me anymore I'm gone. A controlling and manipulative relationship is not of God. You should complement each other, not compete against each other. Some of you are serving in a relationship that is toxic. You're serving in a relationship that is causing you pain and hurt. You're serving in a relationship for co-dependency. You're serving in a relationship because you were hurt as a child and you stay in the relationship due to the insecurities inside.

I dealt with a lot of disappointments in my second relationship. I was in the battle of my life mentally in my 20s and 30s. My expectations in my second relationship were two people coming together, knowing that in order to succeed we must first believe that we can. This was what we both wanted as we came into this relationship at 26 years old already having children by other people. He had a daughter with another woman, and I had a son with another man. His daughter's mother resided in another state with her, and he lived in Queens, New York. Of course that was a part of him that was missing something in his life that he never really got a chance to experience.

Meeting a young lady like myself from Suffolk County who was already independent and on my own, he looked at me as a woman with stability who took very good care of her child. When I think back, I know now our relationship was a little bit too much for him. I was a lot more mature, and already had a certain parenting skill set, obtained from the birth of my son. He was a father as well who loved his daughter very much, but his daughter was not in his life. She was raised by her mother, so he really didn't understand what it was like to be a full-time parent.

He wanted to be a part of his sons world after we had a child together, . It was a very, very difficult pregnancy. I had to inject myself with needles for nine months so that I wouldn't have a premature birth. So once again I put my child first, and I did everything that I had to do to bring my son into the world safely. In the beginning of our relationship he was very charismatic, and being from Queens he had a different approach than some of the guys I knew in Suffolk County.

He became very overprotective of me and our son. He knew how to manipulate a woman by telling her everything she wanted to hear to reap the benefits, and that was my downfall at my age. I believed him. I expected people to treat me in the same way I treated them, and that just wasn't the case with him. It was manipulation in the situation, and the relationship, to get what he wanted, as opposed to us being on the same page and growing in life together. I was with him for a few years.

I left Suffolk County where I established a life for me and my son. I shouldn't have done that, but I wanted to have a family at 26 years old. I wanted us to live in the same house, and since it didn't work out with my first son's father, I wasn't going to do it again with my second, so I proceeded to move to Queens. I shouldn't have taken myself and my first son out of our comfortable situation.

I learned a lot about myself during that time. I think the situation happened so quickly, and there was a demand for a shift in maturity in the relationship and he was not ready for that. I had already established so much security for me and my first son, and then to be pregnant and become a mom to a second son, I was expecting him to make all the moves. It turned out that I was the one making all the plans, and looking for the place. It got to the point where I was like "Ok when are you going to get it together?" We discussed being married before having a child together because that was something that the both of us experienced and we didn't want to do that again. But it didn't work out that way and it ended up being the other way around all over again.

I realized I was attracting the same kind of person with a different face. I began to idolize this man more than God. The truth is, I was attracting this magnet to myself. I really didn't have anyone else to blame but myself. I had very low vibration and self-esteem back then. I was depressed, cheated on, unhappy and insecure, and I didn't know my worth after having two children. Now a second relationship was declining. These men were attracted to my independence like a magnet, but couldn't handle their role in a committed relationship. So of course we talked about our relationship, and those talks led me to believe he was never going to be prepared to be a father full time. or in a committed relationship with me. He had no intention of being under one roof together; it just wasn't what he was used to with his first child. And that frustrated me.

My doctor ordered me to go on bed rest because I was passing out at work. I went on bed rest six months into my pregnancy. During this time I was cheated on, lied to and completely taken advantage of. He would stay out late, not come home, and text other women and disrespect me. I started getting worried. A child was coming into the world in three months and our situation was reckless.

My life changed. I was supporting myself and there were no guarantees this man was going to hold us down. I kind of knew in order for me to have a healthy baby full-term, there were severe sacrifices that had to be made. I had to make some hard decisions . I continued to move forward no matter what the circumstances had looked like. We finally moved in together. I was officially a resident in Queens. Deep down I knew it wasn't a decision that I wanted, and I really shouldn't have made. It's amazing how life works. You can plan your life to be whatever you want it to be, but if it's not what God has planned for you, it will never be permanent. It will only be a chapter in a season that God will use to teach you a lesson for His glory and not yours. If you are somebody with a role in another person's life, and you stop playing that role to focus on something or someone else, it's time for you to go. There's no need to make excuses or try to justify the actions of someone else's behaviour, who has proven they don't care about you. I had to move on. I knew my destiny was not tied to this relationship any longer. The relationship ended in chaos, and confusion started.

I found myself in another court custody battle, but this time it was for four years. This man was so mad that I had moved on and started my life all over again. He was destined to try to hurt me. After we split up I had this terrifying experience that really made me wake up in life. I had something to do, so I dropped my son off with his dad for visitation. As soon as I pulled up in Queens, I was approaching a light and this person was flying so fast to make the yellow light in the opposite direction, that they slammed into my car. They were going so fast that it spun around and hit a pole, causing multiple other cars to collide. All of the gas and oil was leaking out of my car. I thought the car was going to set on fire. The fire department and the ambulance had to come and pull me out of the car. I thought I was going to die when my car was spinning around. I thought to myself this is it for me. I literally thought I was going to die that day. My son was still a baby, only 8 months old and still in diapers. God spared my life that day and it completely changed the way I thought about my future after that accident.

It's so important to embrace who you are in every season of your life. When you have children, your life has to be big enough to make you want to soar, and make you want to exceed past your own expectations. You cannot force a situation or a relationship into your life if it wasn't ordained by God. What I mean by that is, when a situation or relationship is forced, it is your flesh that is causing you to be unhappy. I allowed myself to be in relationships that turned out unsuccessful, but the one thing that I got out of that experience was growth.

When God is not a part of your life, it's always going to be something that you want in your life. Your choices will always be controlled based on the decisions of your flesh and not God, but it becomes a temporary chapter for you and a part of His plan for your purpose. When you decide to take control and not include Him, this causes the delay. God is an amazing God. He loves you so much that He will use every single traumatic, awful painful experience that we go through for His glory even if it may take years. For some of you, it may take many years of your life to fall down and to keep repeating the same cycle over and over, until you finally surrender to Him. Eventually you will realize you have to let go of the things that are hurting you, and causing you pain, doubt, disappointment, addictions, trauma, insecurities and mental illnesses.

IDOLS: Son of Man these men have set up idols in their hearts and put wicked stumbling blocks before their faces should I let them inquire of me at all" (Ezekiel 14:3).

The ultimate measure of a man, or someone that you're in a relationship with, is not worth idolizing over your relationship with God. It's not where man stands in the moment of light comfort and convenience, it's where he stands at times of challenges and controversy. It's during the hard times when someone sticks around in your life when you know that it's true love, and that they're really meant for you.

Being able to tell my story to help someone else in a mental, physical or abusive relationship gives me so much peace in my heart. If your heart isn't right, God cannot and will not intervene because He gives us a choice. I had to get out of God's way, and it took me turning 40 to realize this. I finally realized I'm not doing this anymore. I'm not letting anybody take me out of my character. I know I'm a powerful woman, but I'm not letting anybody force me to be who they want me to be, as opposed to who God created me to be.

Once I let go of all of the enemies' lies that I thought I needed to hold onto to get ahead in my life, God showed me differently. My obedience to Him started meaning a whole lot more to me than what the world thought about me, what people were saying about me or what people thought about my past. God doesn't lie. People lie. It wasn't until I stood firm and was anchored in His promises that my life completely shifted. God didn't care about my past or the sins of yesterday, for He has always been God. He loves the real you, not the "you" you're pretending to be to please other people.

I caused myself a lot of heartache, and a small stroke at one point, that I didn't even know I had until the doctor informed me. It was from stress and broken focus. When I was admitted to the hospital, they didn't know what was wrong with me. After having a CAT scan it was determined that it was a small stroke that I didn't even know that I had. Glory be to God. Being in that bad relationship caused it.

CHAPTER 4

Created for Love

" With god all things are possible"   *(Mathew19:26)*

"The man had position power, and the woman has influence-power."

It was strange how my husband actually came into my life. He was a beautiful man of Italian and African descent, whom I've never crossed paths with before. But God certainly knew how to make us cross paths for His glory. It was at the most unpredictable and chaotic time in my family. On the day we met, my husband's phone rang and as he picked up and answered the phone, he heard someone taking very strong deep breaths- gasping for air and trying to breathe. So he said, "Hello is anyone there?" My grandfather said while struggling to breathe and talk at the same time, "It's Pastor Johnson. I'm very sick, I can't catch my breath and I need you to come to my house right now and take me to the hospital. I need help getting dressed." My husband dropped everything he was doing as a devoted minister to my grandfather's ministry, and ran over there immediately.

While he was en route to my grandfather's house, he called me. " It's Grandpa. I'm very sick. Meet me at Long Island Jewish hospital as soon as you can. I'm on my way to the hospital." So I asked with a sense of urgency and concern "How are you getting there?" He said, "One of my members from the church is taking me to the hospital. His name is Minister Evans. Here is his number. You can call him to get an update while I'm in the car with him, until you arrive at the hospital." I instantly stopped what I was doing at work. I went to my youngest son's school, signed him out and we drove straight to the hospital. God truly works in mysterious ways. We serve a God who will turn your life upside down to get your attention. It's amazing how life is completely under His control at all times.

I approached the hospital. I pulled my vehicle up to the valet and I ran up to the entrance for help to get input on his location to see what was going on. Thank God we had a family member who worked at the hospital as an RN where he was admitted. She was able to give me specific details on what could have been going on. This is a hospital that my grandfather retired from after working there for over 30 years. Because of those connections, he received immediate attention when he checked into the hospital.

It wasn't good news. Unfortunately his kidneys were failing at the tender age of 80. I walked into the room and my husband was standing over my grandfather, praying for him to get through this and be ok. Now again this is a man I've never seen before in my entire life . I am two years younger than him. I later discovered his grandparents and my grandparents were very close as we were growing up because they were pastors as well, but somehow me and him never met. God had a way of preserving this man for my future while I was living in the world.

My husband was raised in a Christian denominational family. His grandparents raised him to be a man of God with a humble and loving persona which was one of respect and loyalty. His character and Christian demeanour filled the room that my grandfather was laying in. I walked into the room with my son and stood beside his bed and I instantly felt purpose, peace, healing, love and support standing on both sides of his bed. My husband and I were facing each other.

At this point a few other family members had arrived at the hospital, and my husband lead us in prayer. We held hands and prayed for his healing, And as we prayed for God's presence to surround that room, a sense of relief was lifted from our spirits. I knew that night I wasn't going to lose my grandfather, and I didn't. He is still pastoring and preaching at First Church Of God In Christ today. It took a lot of treatment. It took a lot of blood tests & dialysis, but he is here today by the grace of God.

That was the most devastating experience with my grandfather that had ever happened in my life. My entire family went into a state of panic because we all live in separate states, but those that were able to be there with him the day it occurred, were a part of Gods purpose. I believe that sometimes God doesn't answer our prayers because He understands how powerful the principle of faith is, and He knows what we're asking for wouldn't be good for us at that time.

We're passionate about wanting God to speak to us and resolve the situation immediately, but God doesn't answer us because It's not a part of His will for our life. After being admitted my grandfather was there for about two weeks. He was able to go home with full instructions to start dialysis to preserve his life immediately, and our family continues to celebrate many more years of his life to come as the Pastor and Superintendent of our district. Currently he's driving himself around and running errands on a daily basis. He's breathing just fine, talking better than ever and preaching every Sunday saving souls that walk through our church doors broken.

After he was released from the hospital I went to his house to check on him. We sat down, we talked about his experience and how devastating it was to me and our entire family, as well as his lead minister who is now my husband. I asked him "Who is that guy in the hospital who prayed for you?" He said to me, " That is Minister Evans. He's a minister in my church. He's been a member for two years. He is devoted and dedicated to our ministry, and he's a wonderful young man." So I said to my grandfather, "I've never seen him before." My grandfather said to me, "Maybe you need to come to church a little more. He's a man of God. He's not married and he doesn't have any children." Then he said, "I think you should go on a date." Now in my mind I did think this man was handsome and I did like that idea, but I said to him "Grandpa don't say anything. I have his number. I'll take the initiative to reach out and thank him." But of course he ignored me and went to church and said something to him.

After service was over my grandfather said to him, "What do you think about my granddaughter?" My husband said, "Well pastor I think she's a wonderful young lady." My grandfather said to him, "You should connect with her and go out on a little date. It was over once my husband got approval from his Pastor and leader of our church. He called me immediately and said, "I just wanted to let you know that your grandfather is doing well. Good and able and he is in church today and he looks great." I immediately thanked him for taking my grandfather to the hospital, being there for him and lifting up all of our spirits. He prayed such a powerful prayer over his life. I told him, " I don't think you understand but you changed my life. You had a huge impact on his recovery." From that moment on we began getting to know each other.

Our relationship just took off like a rocketship. We went on many dates for a few months. My husband told me on our very first date after a few long talks over the phone, "I'm not dating you to be your boyfriend I'm dating you to be your husband." I knew from that moment on that he wasn't just going to be someone that was in my life temporarily. He had intentions of seeking the right woman to spend the rest of his life with. After a couple of months, he just popped the question and asked me to marry him. I said yes and we've been married since 2019.

When my husband asked me to marry him, that's when everything began. After he put a beautiful rock of a ring on my finger, I immediately began to start planning our wedding which was the most precious time of my life. He became very involved between my kids and my husband- taking them out and spending time with them getting to know them both. He knew my boys were the center of my life, so before we became a blended family he wanted to get their approval. It was very important to him that they got to know him and who he really is before the wedding took place. He took them out for brunch several times and they bonded and developed a respectful relationship with them .

My husband didn't want to just come into the situation of someone just marrying their mom and not having a personal relationship with them. He did not move into my house until we were married. He was very intentional about getting my children's blessing before I walked down the aisle, and they respected that. Initially they thought that he was just another regular guy, looking to take my attention. Maybe someone random that I just met and started dating, and now all of a sudden I'm getting married. That was the challenging part because they didn't understand how special this man made me feel. But since it didn't work out with either of their dads, we understood that they were going to give him a run for his money.

Eventually they started to understand how special our relationship was. They saw how kind, loving and gentle my husband was towards me and all of our hearts. Our love for each other did not feel forced. I did not feel awkward and I did not feel like I had to prove something to him. It just felt right.

Of course they didn't see who he really was until we were married and we were a family. He took so much time with my children, getting to know them and getting to know their characters- what they enjoyed and who they truly were. We did family activities with them. We went out to dinner often as a family. We ate dinner together in our home as a family, and he slowly just got into their hearts and their minds and truly discovered who they were intellectually and individually. Most importantly, he made them understand who God was, and how important he should be to them.

My children saw me going to church with my husband constantly, and when they saw the change in me spiritually it opened their eyes to who he really was. Here he is, a man with no children, and now a part of our life.

But immediately he made so much effort and we just became this beautiful blended family naturally. Every day I wake up and thank God for sending me someone like him to share my life with.

So my husband and I proceeded to plan our life together. We have a wonderful family and thoughts of maybe starting our own together. However the crisis in my life continued because obviously the devil knows my potential more than I do. I had a miscarriage because of the previous complications from my past, and now at the older age of 40. I had to revisit the same position I was in at 26. It felt like the same thing was happening all over again.

In the end we realized it wasn't the right time for us and our family, and my husband assured me that God does things in His own timing. We accepted the fact that it wasn't the end of the story as far as us having a child together. It just wasn't the right time. God had something else in His plans for us. My purpose and destiny will be preserved in the future, but at that moment it wasn't time for me to be pregnant again. From then on we continued to push on and just live life and continue to build together and prepare ourselves for the next seasons. We put more into God, and decreased less of ourselves by serving and helping people that need us.

My husband is a giver. He loves to help people. He loves to assist the elderly. His grandparents raised him and they raised him to be a phenomenal man in the absence of his parents. I think because of the way he grew up in that environment he just has a niche for all people.

There was a significant difference in my life after I met my husband. My life of war was just based on me making permanent decisions over temporary emotions, and I was a lot younger expecting the same kind of love I was giving to other people. I was always a daddy's girl, but when my parents separated it was hard for us to build a relationship until I was in my teens and my father became more consistent in my life. He knew I was growing up and becoming a young woman, and he wanted to be my protector. My dad was there for me when I gave birth to both of my children, and his grandchildren love him very much. Although I was predominantly raised by my mom, my dad is my ride or die as well.

My mom and I are very close to this day. She holds a very special place in my heart. I confide in her and she knows every part of my being, and the woman I've become. Like any young girl, as I started getting older I gravitated more towards my peers than to my mother. She had my brother and my little sister to look after, and they were a lot younger than me so I spent most of my time with my friends. My stepdad came into the picture when I was 16 years old. He and my mom got married, and they've been married now for over 20 years.

Now the distinct difference between me and my mother is that I'm a little bit more determined than my mother was when it comes to my dreams and the vision I have for myself. No matter what I go through, I will crawl my way from the bottom and get back up. I'm a fighter. I truly believe there is no success without sacrifice. Many of you may think sacrifices are too costly. You may feel like you're giving up too much. For example spending time with your family may be more important to you than creating a legacy for them. My goal has always been to break the generational curses in my family so my kids don't have to go through what I went through. Surrounding myself in rooms with the like-minded individuals who have dreams and visions to make something of themselves, encourages me to want more than I ever had.

My mother is and will always be a wonderful person. She has a great heart and she loves her family with all that she is and has within her, but at some point she lost herself as well. Although she had me first, separated from my dad and then later had my brother and sister with their dad, she experienced the same thing I experienced. She too became disappointed and discouraged early in her teens and 20s as well, and eventually realized that the man she had two children with didn't want to be with her.

My mother was a strong woman raising us. She did what she had to do to take care of us, and God blessed her with my stepdad. She finally met someone with no children, just like my husband who was also a hard-working man. She got married when I was 16, so the purpose and plan for her life were ordained the same way mine was, but I believe she stopped dreaming after that. At the same time, I was gravitating towards what I wanted to do in my own independence as opposed to what was going on in my household. So the difference between my past and present situation is that I'm more grounded. I'm more confident, I'm more self-reliant, I'm more educated and I'm more focused. I'm not leaning on broken focus. I'm not leaning on being hurt. I'm leaning more on God and focusing forward. My obedience to God is my priority every day.

So yes things were different, but our mistakes help us grow and make us strong, when we get over them. We can make better decisions but they don't define who we are. We can't be defined by our own mistakes because we are human and God speaks to us through those errors in our lives to help us be better people.

I can remember a time when I was leaving my second sons father, and I was just so broken I had finally had enough. I thought to myself it was really time for me to do me again. It was time for me to find myself and my identity prior to bringing any man into my world. I loved my life as a young girl. I loved the athletic side of myself. In high school I enjoyed: music, art, networking, fitness, business, swimming, dancing, reading, and educating myself in fashion, beauty and cosmetology. At one point I wanted to be a model. I was always into myself, and just being the best me that I could be.

I realized years later that I had completely forgotten about who I was, and I had gotten into relationships with men who I idolized more than God. In the end, it really made me want to break out of fear and express what I was feeling on the inside. Why? Because God has big plans for me here on earth. I have kingdom work to do! I was built for such a time as this, and nobody can stop it unless you let them. I always knew I was beautifully and wonderfully made. I just had to start saying it out loud to myself.

The power of affirmations is so incredibly important because life and death are in the power of the tongue. God can't heal what you won't reveal. I had to keep saying to myself, "You are above and not beneath. You are the head and not the tail. You are the lender and not the borrower. Your powerful, you're a leader and not a follower. This is your time."

When you're going through tough times in your life, you need to surround yourself with people who will pull you up towards God. If you're pulled away from God, you begin to believe that you're not capable of anything and you're not able. You're not attractive anymore, you're not the same person you used to be. No one wants you after having children or a divorce, but that is a lie from the pit of hell. That is a distraction from the devil to make you doubt your capabilities.

If that is your reality, you need to look at yourself in the mirror and say I'm not going to stay here in this dark place anymore, feeling sorry for myself in this negative space or relationship with someone I don't want to be with. This is not my reality. This is not where my life stops. This is just a season, because my destiny is not connected to my past. I promise you when you stay anchored in God's promises, you will start to think differently. When you really know who you are, it brings you to a place where you are finally able to leave the past mistakes in the past, and move on knowing those challenges were used for your elevation.

Elevation requires separation. Every ending has a new beginning. Being in court for many years over custody and having a man in my life who was trying to ruin me was difficult, but I understood that he was broken. I truly believe that he was broken and still is. He couldn't deal with the fact that I moved on with my life, and became the same woman that I was when he met me after I left him. I believe he couldn't deal with my strength, and it caused him to turn our lives into turmoil. It cost him to use our son as a pawn to benefit himself by keeping me in court for so many years, but I have so much joy today because as a woman of faith I know this is what you have to go through when God has a purpose for your life. It is a part of the process, and I trust the process. I trust God's will for my life.

CHAPTER 5

Walk in Faith

"She speaks with wisdom, and faithful instruction is on her tongue"(Proverbs 31:26)

I truly believe that my calling in my future resides in ministry, and the life coaching that I have built from that. And I believe whatever you hold in your mind on a consistent basis, is exactly what you will experience in your life. The mind is a very powerful thing, but you have complete control over it. I choose to go higher over evil. I hold things in my heart true and dear on a daily basis, and I ask God every day to use me as a vessel to help someone else overcome the same challenges in life that I had to overcome. A lot of things like confusion, depression, drama and anxiety come from the works of the enemy.

FEAR is: false evidence appearing real. All of these things are distractions to create doubt in your mind. Half of the time the things we think that are going to happen in our lives never even transpire. So now take that knowledge and try to train and coach people in the right direction. Stay connected to the right people that will pull you up and not down. We all have an assignment from God, and that is to serve and to help other people in desperate need of deliverance. Explore the different options in your life knowing that it's OK to take a chance to step out on faith and to let God be God. Many of you don't realize you hinder your growth elevation and purpose when you don't get out of His way! Don't miss your purpose here on earth!

I consider myself very lucky. I'm very appreciative that I have a husband who is able to help me, my family, the elderly and our community. We will continue to do kingdom work together. The assignment for us is to coach others through our ministry, as well as young men and women struggling through life by sharing experiences and information and teaching God's word.

The Lord touched my spirit and He told me to open my mouth and use my voice to help other people, so I started a podcast called Glory Carrier. You can find me on any social media platform and I will get you unstuck. When God gives me instructions I follow. Together my husband and I will have a huge impact in the world. I believe we can touch many hearts as a married couple in ministry helping other marriages succeed. We will preach the gospel while helping people get delivered from the pit of hell and the ways of this world. This book is a part of that.

My husband and I, whether people believe it or not, balance each other out very well. I love the fact that my husband continues to date me as his wife. We prioritize and make time for each other every weekend. We do household activities together, we are very flexible, and we are vigilant about our goals becoming a reality.

My life has completely turned around because of him. God used my husband as a vessel for me to grow in Christ. I started listening to powerful women like RealTalkKim. She was a guest speaker at Jesus Is Lord Church one night. Her message was so powerful. As soon as she made an altar call I ran up to altar and as soon as she laid her hands on me she said, "The Lord told me to tell you, you are more than your degree stop limiting yourself. You have a hard time trusting but you're gonna be alright. You know exactly what you need to do. God is going to put you in the middle of wolves and you're gonna be the light. elevation requires separation. Your life is about to take off like a slingshot. You're about to meet the reason why God would not let you settle. You are a trailblazer."

My life was never the same after that night. I would lie in bed on fire for God with a desire to seek His face. After my husband graced himself into my life I kept my interest in things and people that uplifted me. I did a transformation and complete shift. I suddenly stopped drinking apple martinis. I knew God was delivering me and my mindset was shifting. I hated when people called my phone to gossip about someone because anything routed through my ear to me was a distraction. If it wasn't helping me be a better me, I didn't want to hear it. When you listen to gossip or entertain it, you are no better than the person gossiping. God teaches me how to be silent in frustrated seasons. The less I say, the more He moves. Stay silent around negative people and remove yourself from their energy.

I hope that my book will touch the lives of a variety of people. People who are truly and genuinely seeking deliverance from the ways of this world, and things that are pulling them down. I have young cousins, aunts, uncles and a generation of women in my family from the age of 16 to 80. I would like to see my testimony helping any woman, man or teenager growing up in a house with a single mom or dad like I did. I would like to see my book helping parents who have children and don't know which direction they're going in after a separation or divorce. I would like to see my book helping someone who is a complete introvert with so much potential, and who doesn't even know how to tell anyone how they feel or who they want to be. I want it to help someone who can't even begin to think of how to take the necessary steps in life to open up and to step into their calling.

I think this is the season right now in 2022 for everyone to wake up and find their identity, for people to understand that you're going to go through things in life but you're not going through them alone. There's someone in the world to help you overcome the challenges. There are billions and billions of people in this world and Not everything that you see on social media is what someone's life really consists of. Many of you are suffering and going through very similar situations and living your life covered up with a mask. Some are: severely depressed, dealing with the hurts of your parents, dealing with addictions to numb the pain, dealing with parents who are alcoholics, dealing with loved ones who are on drugs, dealing with being molested, dealing with being raped, dealing with being homeless, dealing with abuse, and a multitude of all the challenges that life throws at people as they walk their life path. And that is absolutely not to say that those are any of the things that have happened in my life, but if this is you, then there is someone who can help you out of your pain.

There is always someone willing to listen. There's always someone who is willing to direct you into the right path, give you the right coaching, the right advice and the right guidance that you need. There is always someone there to give you the support needed for you to persevere, and to step in to your calling because it is real. Every day is a new day to be a better day than yesterday. This is the season for us to take this seriously.

God uses people with the worst past and creates the greatest futures. The great thing about God is that He shows up when you least expect Him. I didn't expect to meet my husband when I went to the hospital to see my grandfather when he was sick. That blew my mind when I thought about how powerful God is. It's so interesting that success is most often achieved by those who know that failure is inevitable.

I am just speaking from my own experience. I encourage everyone to remember to celebrate the milestones that you face as you prepare for the road ahead, because it is not a sentence. You will not go through that situation forever. It's just a season and a test from God. Sometimes God has to cause us pain to bring us closer to Him. He is testing your strength to see your willingness to abide by His will for your life as opposed to your own. He is your Creator. He is your provider. You have the same power instilled in you that Jesus does. The more you praise your way through obstacles and celebrate your life, the more you know that there is something greater on the other side of what you see at the moment.

Right now, I'm in a season of my life that consists of a lot of business, so I consult God in every area of my life-especially as it concerns where I'm going in life in the future as an entrepreneur. He leads me, He guides me, and with the blessing of the Spirit, He will protect me.

I'm 42 today. I'm completely confident in who I am. I know that God has so much more in store for me. This is the beginning of a new chapter for my husband and I as we reap the benefits of obedience. If God can trust you with the small, He certainly will bless you with the abundant. That's why I really don't focus too much on what people think about me or how they treat me anymore. You can't focus on what other people say. People will talk whether you do good or bad. Someone will always have their own perception of who they think you really are, but who cares. God has the final say.

Plant yourself on higher ground and be the best version of you that you can be. You have to treat people with the heart that God gave you , not the heart that He hasn't delivered them from. Create positive energy in your life. Be intentional about your day when you wake up in the morning. Try not to focus so much on what's going on around you in your environment, but focus more on creating a positive energy into your mind. Shift whatever negative energy that comes to your thoughts, and think about something positive to enhance your productivity. What's the point of worrying about things that you have absolutely no control over.

The one thing you can control is your mind. The key to a renewing of the mind is positive energy vibration in your environment and positive thinking. Incorporate some form of working out into your day; it increases the amount of endorphins in your brain to a positive state. Whether it be 15 minutes of walking on a treadmill, jogging, or high intensity interval training, anything positive that makes you sweat and release stress is worth incorporating into your lifestyle. Get some fresh air. Go outside and breathe the air of life into your body. God blesses preparedness.

My goal is to always set an example for my children to be able to break generational curses in my family, and not to have them go through the same things that I went through. I have a big family; my grandmother has four daughters and all of my aunts have children. My cousins are in their 20s and mid 30s, so my goal for writing this book was to set an example not just people all over the world, but for my family also. I want to be that voice of reason, and to encourage them to lean more towards their dreams, goals and vision. It's important for people to understand God's Word. The will of God is in the word of God, and the word of God is the will of God. So embrace what you visualize and dream about, because it's God who is putting that desire in your heart.

In the future I want to expand my services with life coaching both nationally and internationally. I want to use my abilities to reach out to people all over the world on all social media platforms, not just in my community and state of New York. People are desperate for healing and direction today, so my expansion outside of my community and my church will become a priority for everyone. I have truly surrendered my life to God, so I let Him lead me in the direction He wants me to go. I will never proceed to move forward in my life off of my own will. My prayer every day is that God leads me to the right people, and continues to connect me with those that I can inspire.

There are so many women that inspire me in ministry. Today my goal is to share my testimony and set other people free. If you are someone reading my book, and you are ready to set yourself free from the things that hurt you from the past and pulled you down, and made you feel less of who God created you to be, just know God is making a way for you. Stand still and see the salvation of the Lord. Today's the day for you to stop soaking in your sorrows and get up. Rise up kings and queens and push your way through. Don't give up! God's got you. You're gonna be alright!

Unfortunately my family has been spread out in different states for many years now, however , my husband and I are in New York City loving life. When I think back to all of the years of my life being so engulfed in relationships in my 20s and 30s, as well as being a mom, I was in and out of different churches. I see why God allowed every one of those obstacles to happen to me. The crazy thing is, it never crossed my mind that my life wouldn't turn out to be the way I wanted it to, until now.

My son and I got baptized on October 9, 2021. The funny thing is my birthday is September 10, so the day I got baptized is my birthday reversed. It was funny how the day was set up for the baptism and I didn't even realize it, until the day I got baptized. I testified before the church about how God ordained the day that it would happen. I was never baptized as an adult especially after having two children out of wedlock, so that day literally resonated deep in my soul. My oldest son had decided to get baptized because he was just feeling like there were so many signs presenting itself to him repeatedly, and he felt like it was just time for him to give his life to Christ. When I got the phone call that he was going to be baptized, I told him "I will get baptized with you." It was the most precious thing that we have ever done together, and I will never forget it.

The power of a praying woman is real because I was praying for my children's deliverance. I was praying for God to allow this to be a season of revival for them, that they would become young prophets and preach the gospel. Then this happened. I am so grateful God touched his spirit. My son is an athlete. He plays semi-pro football and he was able to testify about his desire to be baptized, which then turned into about 15 other people his age getting baptized that same day. It was a beautiful day. My husband was so happy he even shed a tear at the ceremony because he couldn't believe the decision our son had made and he was so proud of him. We were very proud parents that day. As we stood there watching him take pictures with his baptism certificate, accomplishing another goal after graduating college and persistently pursuing the will of God.

The enemy tried to attack my son multiple times with disappointments. In particular as an athlete he was trying to finish college, but I told him " Do not give up." Do not give into the enemy. "You can do whatever you set your mind to do" and he did. My son realized he had a better situation than some young men. He wasn't homeless, he had a roof over his head, he had his own transportation, and a mom who gave him the whole downstairs on the third level of our home for himself. I always remind him how blessed he is and how he has to take advantage of the doors that God opens for him; to never give up, stay focused and pursue your purpose every day.

My son is now 23 years old and he is so proud of me. I can tell by the look in his eyes that he sees the change in me, and he respects the fact that I found love in and a good husband to be an example to him and his younger brother. My children will always be my purpose, I do everything for them. It's all about breaking generational curses.

CHAPTER 6

Know who you are

"Be self controlled and alert. Your enemy, the devil prowls around like a roaring lion looking for someone to devour. Resist him, standing firm in the faith" (1 Peter 1:8-9)

So at this point I know God has specifically put me on a path and so that I would stay in my lane and trust Him. I feel like I was set on this path and it came at a certain time where I started to see that He was ordering my steps and I'm at ease with that. Fear is not of God. Fear is a significant hindrance for us to overcome, because it often keeps us from believing we can approach God in prayer. It hinders us from having freedom and confidence. When we pray, we become afraid to ask for anything because we believe that it won't happen. This kind of fear will block your faith and your prayers will be ineffective.

Fear will drain the energy from your body. All it is, is worry without profit. It is believing what the devil is telling you and what other people are telling you rather than what God is saying to you. On the path that God has intentionally put me on, everything has gradually started to fall into its rightful place. It gives me a feeling of growth, maturity and confidence. So if I can do it, you can do the same thing. Expect great things in life as you learn to connect your passion and your purpose. I can say from my past and bad experiences they all happened to shape my character. Life is such a problem-solving journey.

The Bible says bring all of your problems to God, and in doing this your problems will bring you growth. When problems arise, it is not the time for us to shrink as believers, but to activate our steps and to allow ourselves to grow into a new person. Age and experience is what separated me from the desires that I once had, I thank God that I changed my desires from the things I wanted temporarily to sustaining and strengthening myself for a lifetime. I now have a desire and a taste for success, not for drama, fast food, alcohol or toxic relationships. Change your attention. Update your brain to manifest what you want in your environment. I had to regain my dignity for people to respect me. Actually let me rephrase that. You have to regain your dignity for anyone to respect you, whether it's your children, family members, people in your workplace, friends or even in your marriage.

Stay away from people that think you're about to argue every time there's a disagreement. Put all of your requests and petitions before God. When you lose your taste for God you lose power, and God then creates in our lives these uncomfortable situations so we can get back to the heart of someone who answers our prayers. . Staying in my lane puts me in the avenue which God uses to bring flavor into my community, my church, parenting, and flavor into my marriage. This transcends into a legacy of game changers. The flavor of God's love is what distinguishes you from being the stale person you used to be. You see, People were not used to me speaking up, they were not used to me owning my crown, they were not used to me dreaming outside of where they were comfortable seeing me stuck. But I knew a God who has called me to bring flavour to a new generation of women and men in my bloodline. He has called me to serve my community and my ministry with confidence, faith and belief in His power. Find a rhythm of passion that sounds so good to you, and overdose on it. God will never be a God of chaos and confusion; He will bring order in the midst of your drama, depression, your disappointments and doubts. Trust Him!

Some of you reading may be holding secrets that are killing you inside, but God wants me to tell you that there's a calling on your life and it's time to set yourself free. Face that problem and the people who hurt you. Take the burden off your mind and give it to Him. If you are someone who is walking on the earth defensively, messy, stirring up drama, gossiping, mean and salty about who you are, you just gave the devil entrance into your mind to try and destroy you. You also gave the devil entrance into your home to mess with your children, your marriage, your ministry, your business as well as your health.

When you know who you really are, you're confident in yourself, and you have faith in God, then the mess in the middle is just a preview of your future. The mess in the middle of my life wasn't bad for me at all. In fact the mess in the middle started to make more sense to me. For every setback, there's a comeback, and every ending has a new beginning. So I stopped looking for validation. I stopped wanting people to approve my saltiness, and I started saying "I am who God says I am." I can't be the person He created me to be until I get my power back.

Why is it that we believe if we want God to use us that we have to have our lives all pretty and perfect for God. God don't roll like that. He doesn't care about your past or your mistakes. You can come to God totally free in all shapes, ages sizes and colors. Whether you're: black, white, green, blue, purple jacked up, broke busted, on child support, abused, molested, raped, evicted, had abortions, babies out of wedlock, on drugs, no teeth, in jail, bipolar an alcoholic with make up on no makeup on bald headed without your weave or with a receding hairline. He could care less. God says come to me as you are. All He needs from you is a 'yes'. So my goal in sharing my testimony in this book, is to help you get completely delivered, and for you to carry the Holy Ghost within; to guide you and lead you not into temptation but into your purpose.

As a life coach, author, businesswoman, entrepreneur and wife to a husband in ministry and soon to be Pastor, our mission is to shift the trajectory of how we live on earth towards Christ. My dream has always been to create an institute of believers and nonbelievers, who become glory carriers, whom I can teach the same values instilled in me so that they would be unstoppable. I thank God for using me as a vessel to help others maximize their potential and to make their dreams a reality.

God will use a frustrated man or woman as a vessel for your deliverance. Just because you had a child with someone, or a job, or business that you lost and things didn't work out, doesn't mean God can't use that situation for His glory. It's a part of your growth process to get you to the next level to become who you were always meant to be. I believe elevation is on the horizon even during this pandemic. I had to find a way to function around my enemies when I was going through pain, hurting, disappointment and doubt because I didn't see the need to confront them anymore. Just because you don't confront your enemies, doesn't mean you're not being provided for by God. I'm here to tell you when you get tired of being tired, you will serve a notice to your enemies and they will know If I had to forgive you, function and tolerate being around you while you caused me pain, now they will have to function, tolerate and live around you in front of your success. .

People should understand your standards, requirements and boundaries if they choose to be in your life. You have the right to set the tone and environment surrounding you with positive energy for your happiness. That's nobody's choice but yours. Stop settling for things that don't bring you joy. Relationships that don't bring you joy, jobs that don't bring you joy and people who don't respect you. You ultimately have to create boundaries to protect your peace in the world today. It's OK to love people from a distance because when you forgive them, you've already protected your own peace by forgiving them. You're not forgiving them for them, you're forgiving them for yourself.

Why is it that we believe we need resources or connections to make our dreams come true. All you need is God's glory. Only God can give you what you deserve. I had to do a lot of research on words to discover my true character. Because words show up like flesh. The word you speak will be so. The Bible says "Life and death are in the power of the tongue." So the first word I discovered about my character was why the word wise means: prudent, intelligent, sharp and very discerning. I would call myself a Proverbs 31 woman of faith. If your words and emotions don't line up with your faith, you will develop a discouraged weary frustrated spirit and that is not of God. I really didn't know in advance that my dreams were possible until I started writing this book. This is a dream but it started out as a vision.

CHAPTER 7

Gods Purpose

"Christ is the one we proclaim admonishing and teaching everyone with all wisdom so that we may present everyone fully mature in Christ"(Colossians 1:28)

Breaking generational curses in my family became extremely important to me. I wanted to be the first one in my family to surpass normal expectations of many things running through our bloodline. I was raised in a family that was always very judgmental. There were a lot of labels. There was a lot of pretending going on in my family. People were struggling on the inside and portraying themselves to be another way on the outside.

I had people in my family that were alcoholics. My maternal grandmother was married to an alcoholic. He died from cirrhosis of the liver. He was a very good hardworking man who took care of his family financially, but still drank alcohol every single day. As a young girl I remember him coming to my mother's house and giving my siblings and I a dollar while smelling like alcohol. He was a functional alcoholic throughout the week, and on the weekends he would drink heavily.

Alcoholism has to do with a chemical imbalance in the brain. Overtime the brain becomes used to these chemical imbalances. This is why some people become dependent upon alcohol, and why removing it from the body can be a long battle. When someone is addicted to alcohol or drugs, it becomes a part of their life even if they want to stop. As a result a person begins to drink more frequently in larger amounts to reach the same state of relaxation and well-being they felt before. Drinking or drugs then become a result of a person's immediate mood. Many people have different drinking patterns, but the consistency is a result and history of mental illness and severe depression.

I found a different way to cope and it was God who gave me the ability to do that. The worst moment of my life was losing a child at 6 months in my late 20s with my first son's father. I was diagnosed with hypertension preeclampsia and rushed to the hospital. After three days of being in the hospital, I was told they were going to have to give me a caesarean to take him out because there was a risk if I didn't let them deliver him. He lived for 2 months and passed away in the hospital.

After healing from that situation, I am now living on my own in Long Island with both my sons getting on with life as a single mom. My ex took me to court and kept me in court for years. It was extremely egregious to me, but the situation with my son was more painful. The court situation was tolerable, but what my son had to go through wasn't. It's not the typical situation I wanted to be in because there was a million, trillion other things I would rather do with my time than to keep showing up in court. The situation with my youngest son was considerably more painful for him at 15, but there is power in the name of Jesus to break every chain. There is power in prayer and obedience to God.

My oldest son is a semi pro football athlete and trainer. We love to work out together on a consistent basis to release endorphins and stress from the brain, so working out has become a part of our lifestyle. Exercise has always been a game changer and place of peace for me. I always feel so much better after working out in high intensity interval training. It's the best thing to do right in the morning to give me a full day of clarity and productivity because I release all of my tension during a good workout that makes me sweat. I love the treadmill and lifting light weights. Being a little sore the next day is worth it because when I put in hard work, dedication and apply myself, I always see great results with my body; and health and wellness is extremely important to me. During the week I always incorporate working out before I start my day, because it's become a hobby.

I found myself looking back at my younger self and thinking wow if I would've just put myself first before other people and things, maybe things would have turned out a lot different. The truth is, I was lacking self development and I was insecure as a young woman. I'm honestly just so thankful that God's plan was better than mine, because I know my self-worth and it's the best feeling in the world. Nothing and nobody can stand in the way of my relationship with God today. There were so many things going on in my life in my 20s and 30s that were right in front of my face, but the crazy thing is I was ignorant to what God was placing before my eyes and I completely ignored all of the signs. When I wanted to do something I did it regardless of what anybody had to say. I really didn't care what anybody thought about the decision I made to be in those relationships with my children's father. And I learned later at the cost of my happiness, that although God was with me through it all, it ultimately was my choice that caused the unhappiness.

My youngest son has a special place in my heart. It took a lot for me to bring him into this world-a beautiful healthy child with so much charisma, character and humour. I don't know, but for some reason when children turn into teenagers they become a little bit more challenging and rebellious. If you're a parent with a teenager I'm sure you can relate. My mom always used to tell me and my siblings to enjoy being kids, because being an adult comes with a lot of responsibility. These kids today just don't understand that. But I always explain to my son who he is, and how important he is to me, and nothing and no one should come in between that. When you let other people put their hands on your mind, you give them the power to be who they want you to be and not who you really are.

"Fathers, do not exasperate your children; instead bring them up in the training and instruction of the Lord". Ephesians 6:4

The one thing that I ask myself as a woman of God with two sons and as a parent with purpose is, "Did Jesus have an adolescent problem? The answer is simply: no. Why? Well one simple reason is that His purpose was reinforced by His earthly father and mother from birth. God wants all parents to know Him so well that they would have an idea of the life and purpose of their children. When you discipline and correct your child, you are giving them a value system for their entire life. It's very important to observe these young people today who have a little sense of direction and morality. This is serious business! Thank God I know that neither one of my children are people who would intentionally do things to hurt other people, but many of you have experienced these seasons in your life, so it's important to be alert and aware of other people. When people claim to love you or if they are a friend or a family member in your life, they must know that nobody should be able to change who God created you to be - especially if it requires you to lie, cheat or steal.

The one thing my husband always tells me, is that one of the reasons he chose me as his wife was because of the love, attention and nurturing that I gave to my sons. He considered them to be so blessed. Before we got married, he knew that I was an excellent mom and he was so impressed with the structure and the responsibilities that I had on my own. As a single mother, the life that I created for them by myself made him so happy that God allowed him to be a part of our lives.

There were a few challenges in the beginning when my husband came into the picture. My kids were very overprotective of me primarily because we were by ourselves for so long, and they were used to being the only males in the house. I never really had anyone around my kids, unless they were worthy enough to be in my kids' presence. I wasn't the kind of mom to bring random men home into my home around my children. I just wasn't that kind of person. My kids always came first, so it took a couple of months for them to get used to my husband being my fiancé, and eventually they grew to like and appreciate him for being the good person he is to us. Today they love him so much and we're a well blended family.

Sometimes when we have family nights at home and they tell my husband, "We didn't think you had a chance when you first met mom, now look at you. You certainly knew how to prove yourself right and us wrong." So they really appreciate him and the fact that he treats me like a queen. It makes me happy they truly understand now that they're older, just because it didn't work out with their dads which is something that I was destined to accomplish, doesn't mean that we both don't love them very much. It just means we weren't supposed to be together forever and that's okay.

CHAPTER 8
A Renewing of the Mind

*"God is our refuge and strength an ever present help in trouble,
therefore we will not fear though the earth give way and the
mountains fall into the heart of the sea, though its waters roar and
foam in the mountains quake with their surging" (Psalm 46:1-3)*

As I was writing this book the word activate came to my spirit. Activation occurs as we practice God's presence consistently in our lives. God is consistently enlightening our hearts to see His face, so we just have to prioritize Him to be the center of our life. it's almost like having a gym membership and going to the gym to lose weight. You're committed to eating the right foods, but you have to set your mind and keep it set on reaching your goal to see a change in yourself. It's always a good idea to set your mind on something that is good for you because you're never going to get the results that you're looking for without renewing your mind. It has to be a lifestyle that you stick to, and hold yourself accountable for on a daily basis.

The way I did it was to subconsciously think about the things that I had to do to change my life. I had to subconsciously think about all the things that I was doing that no longer served me any good, and I want you to do the same. Ask yourself as you're reading today, "Is there anything in my life that I can do to make me a better person? Then write it down!" "And the Lord answered me and said write the vision make it plain upon tables that he may run that readeth. For the vision is yet for an appointed time, But at the end it shall speak, and not lie, though it tarry, wait for it, because it will surely come, it will not tarry" (Habakkuk 2:3)

Many of you spend so many hours a day doing things that don't serve you any good, scrolling on Facebook or Instagram when you could be seeking your purpose by giving God your time. These are some of the things we need to acknowledge in 2022. You don't have time to give the devil entrance into your lives or your children's lives anymore. Decisions must be made about how you can make a difference in the world. How can you help someone else get from under the pit of hell? How can you save a soul and bring them to Christ? How you can make yourself some more money as an entrepreneur? How can you teach your children to expand their minds and be the best version of themselves God created them to be? This requires making the decision to take action now rather than later.

The young children in this generation today are no longer the same way they used to be in the 70s 80s and 90s, where they played outside and came home when the streetlights went off . These kids today act as if they're adults. As teenagers, they become more of a threat to their parents, than their parents are to them. And what I mean by that is, teenagers today try to control their parents more than their parents control them. They see taking cell phones, video games and laptops away as a form of abuse and are quick to involve police and a court system.

Prayer was initiated. Prayer had to be my priority because as for me and my house we will serve the Lord .I had to practice this exercise by saying to myself aloud, I'm going to dedicate and set a time aside every day for God. I'm going to pick a place of prayer in my home where I am isolated from the busy ways of the world, and the busy ways of life, and I'm going to dedicate this time for myself and God to have an intimate relationship.

And that applies during my work week as well. I make time to pray every three hours during a specific realm and hour of the day from 6 AM all the way through the rest of my day. Why? Because my prayers have a specific effect in the spiritual realm. We are living in the last evil days, and don't you think for one moment that you can survive in this world without God and your prayers. The enemy comes to steal, kill and destroy. Pray for your children, pray for your family, pray for the church, pray for your pastor, and if you don't have a church that you go to every week you better find one. Get into a church that is on fire for God and serve in ministry. If you're a grandparent pray for your grandchildren. Pray in the spirit every chance you get. Knock the devils teeth out. Prayer must be a conscious decision that you make to specifically give God your time. No one really has to know exactly what you're doing but you and God. God blesses obedience!

Becoming a life coach was something that I decided to do after my experiences and life took me on a roller coaster ride. I realized that I needed more experience. I also needed more discernment. I needed more wisdom to be able to share with others, so I decided to become a life coach after getting my Bachelors degree in Business Management and Communications. This was a decision made after I got married to my husband and I started to live a life that actually started to make sense. I was making God a priority. I have been separated from my ex for over 10 years with whom I have my second son with, and it all just started to make sense- education is knowledge and the more knowledge you have the more people you can help. I started to surround myself with people that uplifted me. The more rooms that you step into that are filled with success, the more your desires will grow. I invested in my future and put myself in an environment towards elevation. The more knowledge you have the more you can share with other people.

So I started to have a conversation with God every day the same way I have conversations with people. He's like that best friend that you always pick up the phone to call when you break up with your boyfriend, or a family member or who you talk to about your marriage or even your husband that you talk to you when you're feeling down or you need to be uplifted. God should be your focus over all of that or any of that. I chose to give my problems to Him, to surrender to Him to see me through the trials and tribulations of my life because the battle was not mine it was His. "The Lord shall fight for you, and ye shall hold your peace. (Exodus 14:14)

When I started to do that, things started to make a lot of sense. That's not to say that there weren't obstacles in between what I had in mind for myself, and for the future. Because He had already had my future planned but I had to figure out how I was going to operate on a daily basis. "Our Greatest weakness lies in giving up." The most certain way to succeed is always to try one more time never give up" -Thomas Edison

My decision to get an education was basically an effort to break generational curses because my parents don't have a college degree. That was something as their first born child that I was determined to do. Not just for them, but to break generational curses for my children, so they would understand that you can do anything that you put your mind to when you separate yourself from the ways of the world. It has nothing to do with where you came from, what you experienced and what you've gone through. It just has to do with you! So my children became my "why." They were the reason why I decided to get my degree, and although it was tough as a single mom, I'm here to tell you, the number one rule to remaining strong is never to start something and not finish. You have to set your mind and keep it set on what you want for yourself. Nothing and no one is standing in the way of your dreams and goals becoming a reality.

Whenever I felt there was something that I wanted to do, I consulted God about it. Whenever I was feeling down and needed to be uplifted, God was my focus over anything. I graduated with my Bachelors degree in 2019, and I'm still seeking education and self development daily. The hustle for me never stops. Give your problems and your concerns to God not people, then keep your mouth shut and continue to pray and move on. Every day is a new day, to be a better day than yesterday.

God knows all about your secrets, He knows all about you totally. I know this is through my intimate relationship with God. I know from seeking His face that He knows all your secrets. He knows your heart. He knows all about everything that causes you pain. He knows all about everything that discourages you, causes fear in your heart, gives you anxiety or disappoints you. He knows it all.

I had to take the necessary steps and courses to become a life coach to help other people. It was just something that I felt needed to be an added bonus to where God was taking me. I took these courses online to learn how to life coach other people through life, and it just felt right to me especially during COVID with people living in so much fear. Nothing in my life that transpired was ever a surprise to God. All He wanted from me was a "yes" and "amen" and He wants the same from you. He wants you to accept Him for who He is, and not to rely on yourself. Now we all know from the very beginning in Genesis when God created Adam and Eve, God always gave us a choice. If God doesn't have anything to work with, He cannot align with you and move in your life the way that you need Him to. Why is that? Well primarily because we all have a choice. By faith and independence, you can put off the old nature and stand in victory through Jesus Christ as you put on the new man. Therefore today we have the right to put off the old nature with its selfishness, and put on the new nature with its love. You have the ability to put off the old nature of your life with its fears, and put on a new nature with courage.

I remember becoming a young mom like it was yesterday. I was so excited and nervous at the same time to give birth to my older son, not really knowing what was ahead of us for the future. It became very scary when you rely on your feelings to get you through life because people will disappoint you. People change, seasons change, and we all change, mature and grow at different stages of life.

But I remember one day, I said to myself I must've been in my late 30s at this point because I was always someone who thought I knew everything. Nobody couldn't tell me nothing, especially if I was in love. My family had no success with trying to give me their advice. I didn't care about what anyone thought. I always made up my own mind, and I remember God just letting me do me, but still preserving me to eventually become the woman I am today. I am thankful for His forgiveness. I am thankful for His grace and mercy in my life.

I always had a conscience, I always knew how far to go. I never let myself go all the way there where I was lost and couldn't come back from a place of brokenness and start again. I've always been able to pick myself up through my strength and keep it moving. I knew at some point, well actually God knew at some point, she's going to hit rock bottom and finally submit to me wholeheartedly.

And that was the day I got completely fed up. A few years before I got married, I was in a very dysfunctional relationship with my second son's father and I just refused to stay stuck in that place with him. I was very unhappy. I was very broken and I was at my wits end with life living in Queens, New York. I finally said to myself, I refuse to stay In a relationship that I'm not happy in. I refuse to stay stuck with someone who is with me, but has cheated and already left a relationship. I refuse to believe the feelings that I feel right now permanently. It was time to get into some healing. The battle was too big for me, but it wasn't too big for God.

I held up the shield of faith against all the false accusations in my life I was facing, and against all the insinuations that Satan put in my mind. I claim the fullness of the will of God over my life, and my life literally changed ever since then. It was a decision that I chose to make for myself, to let go and walk away in order for me to be able to move forward. Letting go is such a huge weight off of your shoulders, when you release all the negative things in your mind causing you pain- and refreshing it with nothing but positive visions.

I realize that from a very young age I've learned that if I turn on some gospel music and just praise and worship, then it can get you out of a negative state of mind. Worship is an amazing way to restore your faith, your trust and the power of God into your life. It's also more than just singing, if you listen carefully, the words begin to minister to your soul. I believe Jesus understands every affliction known to man. The Lord gives us a heart to worship consistently. The words of His promises don't necessarily have to explain when a song is over. His promises are forever.

So He promised me from the day before I was even conceived, before I was life at all, when I was a seed in my mom's womb, what my life was going to consist of.

We all have felt demoralized at some point in our lives. We will all reach a point when we lose confidence or hope and become disheartened. There will always be times when life really becomes challenging. God will place a vision in our hearts at some point in time, and as the process becomes challenging and we start to feel discouraged, we may start to second guess if we should continue doing what we're doing. I promise you that's when your breakthrough is actually closer than you think. Don't give up! The Bible says that first comes the famine then comes the provision. God will always multiply what we have and He will provide our needs every day at exactly the right moment.

We really don't have anything to worry about because God's provision will ensure that His will be done. It will be God or it will be God. There are no other options for His will in your life. Stay focused! God's will, will most certainly be accomplished in your life on earth as it is in heaven. God wants us to be planted and anchored in every area of our lives here on earth. Be the difference, be the one to change your family dynamic. Yes I understand it's hard, life is difficult. It becomes hard when you have children. It's hard w

hen you're in a marriage or you're in a relationship that you're not happy in, but the good news is, that's where your strength shows. The kind of strength that you never knew you had, the kind of strength that makes you rise up as a king or queen from a state of confusion, into a sense of direction.

That's when you have to identify who you really are, who you were going to be and why you're here. I had to do that for myself. Nobody is going to do it for you. You have to be willing to find yourself in order to be who God created you to be. Not just for myself but as a parent with purpose with a vision, with my family, in business and in my relationship with God. In 2022 we need to invade spaces and industries and make ourselves relevant everywhere we go, as opposed to just taking up space and staying stuck in areas that we actually don't want to be in. Who really wants to be involved with anyone who doesn't make us feel good? Not just in relationship but even with our jobs, our families our friends, or significant other. The woman I am today senses if you don't want or appreciate me, I'm gone. The more you pay attention to the patterns in your life, the more you will recognize that there is a pattern in your process.

Many of us get off track every single day, and we start looking at what other people are doing over there and over here in the world. It happens at our jobs, in our churches and in our families but we never stop to think about the blueprint of our lives individually. We all have a blueprint to our lives, and when you look at it, there should be some way that you understand how far you've come, and where you're going. That takes "dying to yourself" to let go of the old version of yourself, and to enter into the next season and level of your life as a completely different individual.

I remember a time when many people became jealous of me because God showed me a vision. They were jealous because I saw a vision that He didn't show them, and from that I learned people will always try to judge and hate on you. Hurt people hurt other people, and they will try to find a reason to get others to turn against you without any understanding of a calling on your life. This is what eventually causes your enemies to try and publicly humiliate you, or to shame your character with lies and false accusations. Things like this will happen especially if you are successful. The good news is that nothing and nobody can come between God's purpose and plan for your life, and for the people who don't understand it, that can be very dangerous.

Vision has always been my thing, and making other people believe in their vision is my assignment. I want to help other people become who they really want to be the same way God did it for me. I aim to do this with my life coaching, with my testimony, with my book and with just seeking out and reaching out to anyone in need of help by going out and doing God's work. Kingdom work consists of bringing people to God, bringing people to church, and helping them be freed from the pit of darkness- from those evil forces in their lives that have had them stuck for so long.

CHAPTER 9

The Reflection of Life

"Delight thyself also in the LORD; and he shall give thee the desires of thine heart." Psalms 37:4

I think as we become competent, we have a complete understanding of who we are, what we want, and God's promises. The things that occur in life along the way become very humorous. Whenever an attack comes on my life that's when I begin to rejoice and give God the honour and the praise. Why? because we know there's something on the other side of it. Life is not a competition, it's about individual growth and maturity. It's only as we grow through life that we learn about life! Never feel discouraged or jealous about what another person has, and get distracted thinking about someone else having the perfect life, the perfect husband, the perfect children, the perfect house and or job, because God made all of us individually. He has a plan and purpose for each and every one of us. We are all different, with a different purpose. Seek your purpose. Never desire to imitate who someone is.

Be your authentic self. There will never be another you. Start thanking God for the things that you haven't even seen yet, and that He didn't do yet. That is a sign that you're seeking spiritual growth and maturity, and you're learning in life when you start seeing that you won't desire to do the things that you used to do before. You will desire to create an environment around you that serves your purpose. All of the decisions that you used to make when you weren't following God will just stop, and that will be a sign that you're experiencing spiritual growth and a renewed mind.

It doesn't matter what people think of you. There are things in life that are already prepared for your future that you can't even see yet. And God is over here saying, let people talk. You don't have to say a word. Your fruit will speak for itself. Know that during challenging seasons, you are different. Know that there's an anointing on your life. You were set apart, and were created for a time like this. When you sincerely seek God, there should be a change in your life, there should be a change within you, your vision, and your desire to move forward and to become a better version of yourself. When you learn how to articulate the good, and bad , you will be different in your wisdom and the way you operate. Then and only then will you find your footing in the ground to be able to find yourself again.

There were some things in my life that I had to go through. Things that no doubt were trying to destroy me and the people around me. People will have their own commentary narratives about who they think you are based on who they know you used to be. And that's unfortunate because we live in an evil world. It's a shame that people expect you to be who they know you used to be, and not who you know you were created to be. When someone has a curse on your life and devises a plot, plan or scheme against you, they're going to do it because that makes them feel good about themselves. They have made themselves believe that what they were doing toward you is OK. But I'm here to tell you the enemy cannot win when you use the power of God's Word. Be bold and confident in saying "No weapon formed against me shall prosper and every tongue that rises up against me in judgment shall be condemned."

Never focus on people who want to cause you hurt, harm or danger. I believe I was created to be a category creator, to be someone who has done something that no one else has done before. God didn't create me to mock or be an imitation of someone else. You are fearfully and wonderfully made, and to do you in a unique way for God's glory on this earth. Embrace who you are and your uniqueness. We all have something special about us!

You have to keep in mind that there will be people in your life who are not ready to go to the next level with you. Every level demands a new version of you as well as growth. What you believe changes what you perceive, and the question to ask yourself is: do you really believe

God's love for you? If so, then you need to trust in Him and He will create the hope, and the confidence that you need to move forward.

My husband came into my life at the right time when God knew I was ready to step into a new realm and new level of elevation. We both learned along the way that God will crush your pride and open your heart to love. All we really have to do is let others know that they are not alone and that is exactly what my husband does for me. I'm so grateful to be able to share my life with him. It wasn't until I stopped seeking a man that God sent me the right man.

The manifestation of glory begins this season in 2022! I believe that God is going to let everyone know who He is, as well as who you really are. He has not forgotten all that we've done in our lives, or all that we've been through. He has been our Rewarder for it all. I'm here to tell each and every one of my readers today your payday is coming unexpectedly. There are things that are going to happen in your life in 2022 that will surprise you this year, and blow your mind. Your strength will increase, your confidence will get better, your patience will give you peace, and the people in your life will begin to support you and elevate you. What you are getting ready to birth is already in your hands. Glory be to God, many of you reading today are already walking in your spirit ground, that's why the devil attacked you. I promise you, stay focused and God will take you to the next level in your faith, obedience and walk with Him. Pray in the spirit daily and continue to stir up your faith.

God must be our number one priority in life. I cannot make this clear enough. Do not waste your time trying to explain anything to people who don't have the same wants, dreams and aspirations as you. Stay in the spirit and pay attention to your environment. You definitely have to lose your whole life to begin a new one, so kings and queens I believe this is an exceptional time for elevation. God is going to do exceedingly and abundantly, more than you can even ask or think in this season. He is saying to all of us the last season of our lives may have been difficult, but I was basically teaching you to acknowledge the attacks, because in the season ahead I want you to acknowledge me. So it's not just about putting all of our focus on what's happening to us, playing the victim and not understanding why. God allows so many things to happen to us. It's not about the attacks, it's the acknowledgment of who God is and how He wants us to acknowledge Him. Focus on Him in a time of hardship, not on the devastation of what's being done to us.

If God can use David or Moses He can use you, but you have to know who you are. Some folks will be very apprehensive about who they really are or what they are going to be but it's ok God will humble you through the process. The enemy is always going to try to publicly scandalize you when he knows there's a calling on your life. What actually makes us think that life is going to be this picture perfect place where everything is perfect in all four seasons, and we won't face any adversity. How would that make us grow and learn from our mistakes? It is when we become able to rebuild a new life and re-launch a better version of ourselves that we understand where we're going. It's because of the grace of God on your life. Many are called but very few are chosen.

It doesn't matter if you've suffered from persecution, what you've been through all your life, or how many mistakes you've made in your past. At the appointed time God will change your situation for His glory. It will be God who calls you to build your business. It will be God who places the vision in your heart, and it will be God who places that dream in your mind. For our children, it will be God who tells them to write the vision and make it plain, and to write that book they've always dreamed of writing. These are the desires that we will start to feel in our hearts that will come from God, not man.

When I look back at my entire life, being 42 I can say I'm proud of myself. Everything I went through made me who I am today. I had a war: in my relationships, with progress, with being a dark skin beautiful woman, with getting my foot through certain doors, with knowing that I am beautifully and wonderfully made, with many things in my life that try to take me out. Nothing ever came easy, but I had to make some serious decisions along the way- to be different and not follow the ways of this world.

When you're dealing with a lot of immature people in your life, people who don't understand or see the anointing on your life, they can discourage you. You may start to follow other people thinking that the grass is greener on the other side instead of trusting yourself. Don't ever allow people to demonize your process. You can't Google how to navigate to the next level. It's time to ask yourself: what needs to die in your life, what convicts you and how does it makes you feel? This will help you get to the next level.

This is the time, now more than ever during COVID-19, to get your heart all the way right and to put God first. If you want your thoughts to be right, if you truly want to be transformed and delivered, then you need to die to self. There are so many things on the inside of you that have to go. If you want rebirth and a new life, then and only then will you be completely delivered. Whatever you're still holding onto from your past, surrender to the Lord and let it go. Something in your life must die for the Holy Spirit to live in you! And what I mean by that is, would you ever take something out of the oven before it's fully cooked? Well, the answer is no, right? You would let it fully cook to your liking before you take it out the oven, so that your taste buds are fulfilled.

God has always been a jealous God. He doesn't like it if you put other idols before Him like men, women, friends, work, business, family, children or money. I had to completely accept everything about me and what I thought was the right thing for me, in order to transform my whole entire mind. I had to renew my thinking. I got tired of doing things my way, not getting the results that I expected God to give me. So I knew at one point in my life I wasn't completely delivered. I was the kind of person who said everything for myself. I made all the decisions without consulting God. I just kept skipping through life like everything was peaches and cream, and then I had the nerve to ask God, "Why are you letting these bad things happen to me?" But He's over there saying "You never consulted me."

There were many unexplainable answers to the questions that I was asking myself. Before I got married it was done with the help of the Holy Spirit, and my knowledge as a life coach that revealed certain things to me. The enemy is always going to be on a rampage to bring many lives to an expiration date, and he is seeking to attack people spiritually, physically and most of all mentally.

Many people today are suffering from mental illnesses. They're living unreasonable lives, and some are even taking their own lives because of depression. Violence is at an all-time high, and people are becoming radically dangerous in the streets and in their cars. Hit and runs are all over the news. People are driving around angry and bitter. Young kings and queens are being murdered by police, and people are seeking revenge out of anger, hurt and injustice. Riots are taking place, fights and fires are occuring from city to city, and people are legally allowed to carry guns in some states. So why don't we feel at this point in life, in the year 2022 that we need God? If you don't believe that you're crazy, because He's coming. He's coming back one day, and the revelation is what we're living right now. Needless fights are breaking out everywhere, in concerts and schools. These places are getting shot up and attacked by people, while innocent children are walking the hallways. Pray for a hedge of God's protection over your children's safety every day. Inspire others to lead, not follow.

So I want you to hear me and hear me closely when I say this to you. Pay attention this year. The Lord is going to bring His intent and glory that has been revealed and spoken from loud voices to manifestation. So many people all over the world are going to search desperately for God's counsel which they actually once despised, and they will realize how far from the truth they really are. Spiritually there are dangerous trends of people in the world today serving a God they don't even know. This leads them down a complicated journey attempting to gain freedom. This is a problem, this is a huge problem today!

Because what many of you don't understand is that you can't choose the version of God that you have framed for yourself, and believe that's the true God. This version of Him allows you glorify sinfulness. So instead of repenting of your ways, many people today simply maintain all lifestyles expecting change from God. Humans all over the world have found a risky balance for themselves without any proper standing with God. They continue to live their lifestyles. They create a God that they feel is comfortable enough in their minds to serve, but they still live their own life at the same time. The Bible tells us speak up for those who cannot speak for themselves, for the rights of all who are destitute, speak up and judge fairly, defend the rights of the poor and the needy.

I have always believed in integrity. Integrity is not something that you show others, it is how you behave behind closed doors when no one is looking. I truly believe in integrity. Dogs, have integrity. Humans sometimes lack it! Courage combined with integrity is the foundation of character.

"Whosoever is careless with the truth and small matters, cannot be trusted with important matters" -Albert Einstein

I know for a fact through my experiences and having children at a young age, there is no better test of a person's integrity than their behaviour when they're wrong. I encourage all of my readers to honour your commitment with integrity. Every man must decide whether he will walk in the light of creative altruism or in the darkness of destructive selfishness. As a mom, I will always continue to encourage my children to stay humble. Be who you really are and not who people want you to be.

Most importantly when things go wrong, and sometimes they will, don't ever give up and quit!

CHAPTER 10
Encourage your Children

"But when, He the spirit of truth, comes, He will guide you into all the truth." (John 16:13)

Success is failure turned inside out. It's like dark clouds in the sky that give us doubt. You can never tell how close you are to an unexpected blessing but it never crosses your mind that it might really be very close to you. It may be near when it seems so far. But the only way you will ever know is when you stick it out during the fight, when you stick it out and you're at the hardest point in your life. You'll never know if you quit.

I want to make a difference in other kings and queens lives who struggle with indecisiveness. I have come a long way and I've been through a lot. I have been through many near death situations. I have had children and I have lost children. From experiencing near death situations in life, my message to the world is to learn from those times. Those lessons are not happening by mistake. My assignment is to help people through hard times when they feel like giving up, and don't have anything left to give. When they're homeless, in jail, and in shelters. When they're not knowing where they're getting their next meal from to feed their children. I want to be that voice and say "Get up! Get up! Open your mouth and declare and decree what you want into your life."

It starts with self development. Look in the mirror and tell yourself who you are. Know that you were born for a reason, and the whole point of you being here is for you to discover that. When you do will not allow other people to put their hands on you and your mind. Some of you are living your life for other people because you're insecure. You have fear, doubts discouragement and you've been disappointed and heartbroken. That means you have not gotten over your hurt. If you're still walking on the street broken, and you're still navigating through life by your own will and not God's will, it's a very dangerous place to be-not knowing your true identity or any idea of who you really are and what you want out of life.

God can change your life in a matter of seconds, but you have to be a strong lion. You have to be strong-willed, and a person that knows breakthrough is coming. You have to know when to cut the cord off from your old way of life, whether it's getting off drugs, or whether it's time to stop drinking. You have to know when it's time to stop smoking cigarettes (although I never had issues with any of these things) but everybody is built differently.

Some people are cut from a variety of cloths, and have experienced some traumatic things as a child and well into adulthood.

No person is going to handle things the same way as you. They don't know how to get themselves out of that awful place and they become stuck. But there is always someone to help you through those challenges. Being a life coach allows me to be that voice to help anyone in need. Whether it's through my podcast called "Glory Carrier" an email, Zoom or sitting on my panel, and coming to my church to share their testimony. However you choose to get delivered, stay connected with someone who will pull you up. Get into a good Bible based church on fire for God and get yourself some healing. Deliverance comes from a place in your soul. Life and death is in the power of the tongue.

Many of us don't understand that when we speak things out of our mouths, we're calling those things into our lives. When you speak negatively, you're allowing the enemy into your life. You're allowing these bad oppositions to take place. Speaking doubtfully will only cause those things you fear and worry about to happen. For example, when you say "I can't do this", or "I can't ever buy a home" ,or "I won't ever have a nice car", or "I can't start my own business, I'm broke." The reason it isn't happening has nothing to do with God. Not having your prayers answered has everything to do with your faith. God is not a genie in a bottle. You have to put in the effort to be where you want to be in life, and He will bless your preparation and obedience. Whether it's through giving, tithing or serving in the ministry. But if you're just sitting at home speaking doubtfully, not going to church, not trying to serve in ministry, and being negative, you will stay right where you are- unhappy stuck and in bondage.

You are the only one who can put a limitation on your mind and your future. My hope is that my book will get in the hands of someone in jail. I want it to reach someone who has completely given up on themselves, and sees no reason to be who God created them to be, but deep down inside are a really good person. Someone who can change the world or witness, testimony, but they just don't have that necessary understanding of life. Maybe they didn't have a mom or dad who told him every day that they were beautiful or smart. Maybe nobody has ever said, you can be all that you want to be, you can do all things through Christ who strengthens you. "Greater is He that is in me, than He who is in the world"

It just might be that they didn't have that structure in their home, where they ate supper at a certain time with their moms and dads. Maybe they came from a broken family. Maybe they grew up with just a mom and not a dad, or a dad and not a mom. I grew up with a single mom. I had my dad as I got older, but I grew up in a family where my parents weren't together. My mom raised me. My dad was in my life, but my mom was the primary parent who made all the decisions. So from my experience as a young, innocent child and now being a mother, I see that there is a necessary way that life has to go in order to achieve success-and you don't have any time to waste in between.

If I would have given up in my 20s, I would probably be dead right now. I'm sure there are probably many men and women who have been cheated on and gone through the same drama that I experienced with a young child. But God makes the greatest futures out of people with the worst past. Those are the kind of people I want to see in my church. People who come in wreaking of alcohol, smell like marijuana, desperately seeking deliverance from God. I'm not into fake phony and fickle people. I love them but I love them from the balcony. I'll feed you but you won't sit at my table. My environment and circle of people that I surround myself with are glory carriers and trailblazers. People who are on fire for God, who seek Him daily in pursuing their purpose.

I used to be in relationships that God already knew were only temporary chapters in my life. I stayed in those relationships a little too long because I really didn't have the necessary structure growing up that I really desired. But as a grown woman I knew how to get myself back on track and I began to recognize the desire and the power that was instilled on the inside of me, and that was what it looked like on the outside. I knew if I kept doing the same things making the same mistakes, and living the same lifestyle with others I wasn't happy with, things were going to spiral out of control very quickly. So I became a decision-maker. I set an example for my children that my mom didn't do for me. I had to set an example and broke the generational curse off of my life, by getting my degree, walking away from relationships, environments and people that served me no good, and seeking God's face became my number one priority. Yes that was my goal!

That's how I want to conclude my message to the world. My message to the world is that love never fails. My message to the world is that you can do all things that you set your mind to do. My message to the world is: Don't hold back how you feel inside. Speak about it and if you don't feel comfortable speaking to someone about it, speak to God about it. He will redeem you. He is a redeemer. He will comfort you, He will cover you and He will protect you. You don't have to live this life alone.

Guilt is related to the fear of not being forgiven. Some of you may be living with a constant sense of being condemned by God, and therefore you always feel guilty. However (Romans 8:1 tells us "therefore there is now no condemnation for those who are in Christ Jesus because through Jesus Christ the law of the Spirit of life set me free from the law of sin and its consequence death". There is now no condemnation. This truth is very crucial for us to understand if we are to approach God in prayer. Have you ever been in prayer or worship service and began to remember things you've done wrong in the past things for which you've already been forgiven and cleansed? It will continue to make you feel guilty. Why do you feel this way? It is because sometimes guilt comes from distrust. If you have asked God to forgive you, He has forgiven you. If you are still carrying the sin around in your heart and mind then you are doubting that God forgave you. That is why the guilt comes back to life. The devil uses that guilt to undermine your faith.

When you pray, your faith becomes weak and your prayers are not answered. So I say this to say, you don't have to live in depression, and you don't have to commit suicide. God has forgiven you of your sins in repentance. If you are suffering from mental illness, that's even more reason to read your Bible and stay connected to the Word of God. You don't have to think that nobody loves you, because God more than anybody loves you. Even though you can't see Him. He created you and God wants you to succeed, so that intimate relationship with Him has nothing to do with nobody but you and Him. It is not an embarrassing thing and it's not a spooky thing. It's an intimate relationship that you have established by your own will and offered to God. When you surrender your entire life to God He will do the rest. The Bible says, " If your motives are wrong, your prayers will be hindered. "When you ask, you do not receive because you ask with wrong motives that you may spend what you get on your pleasures (James 4:3)." What are your motives for praying? Are you asking God for something for other selfish purposes or are you asking God to fulfill His word so that His kingdom can come here on earth?

God knows we have needs, and it's not wrong to request that He fulfill them based on His words. Our focus should be on honouring God and promoting His promises. When we have our priorities right, we can trust Him to meet our daily needs. Why? Because Jesus promised us! Therefore I say to you, when you pray check your reasons for praying. Ask God for forgiveness for any wrong motives you may have, and to develop the right motives to do what the Holy Spirit commissions you to do in your life. "For it is God who works in you too well and to act according to his good purpose. (Philippines 2:13)

Made in the USA
Middletown, DE
22 February 2023

25098056R00071